TREVOR NOAH

Biography

BEYOND THE DEFINITION OF CRIME

Dolly Beatrice Robles

CONTENTS

CHAPTER 1

RUN

CHAPTER 2

BORN A CRIME

CHAPTER 3

CHAMELEON

CHAPTER 4

LOOPHOLES

CHAPTER 5

THE MULBERRY TREE

CHAPTER 6

OUTSIDER

CHAPTER 7

GO HITLER!

CHAPTER 8

THE CHEESE BOYS

CHAPTER 9

THE WORLD DOESN'T LOVE YOU

CHAPTER 10

MY MOTHER'S LIFE

ENDING

CHAPTER 1

RUN

My entire family is religious, but my grandmother reconciled her Christian religion with the traditional Xhosa traditions she'd grown up with, interacting with the spirits of our ancestors. For a long time, I couldn't figure out why so many black people had abandoned their original religion in favour of Christianity. Church, or some version of church, was there at least four nights a week during my childhood. The prayer meeting was held on Tuesday night. Wednesday nights were reserved for Bible study. Youth church was held on Thursday night. We were off on Friday and Saturday. (It's time to sin!) Then we went to church on Sunday. I grew up in a household where there was little exposure to popular culture. Boyz II Men was not permitted in my mother's home. Songs about a guy grinding all night on a girl? No way, no how. That was not permitted. I'd walk into school and hear the other kids singing "End of the Road," and I'd have no idea what was going on. I'd heard of these Boyz II Men, but I had no idea who they were. I only knew church music: soaring, uplifting hymns praising Jesus. The same was true for movies. My mother didn't want sex and violence movies to poison my thinking. So the Bible served as my action film. Samson was my personal idol. This particular Sunday, the Sunday I was hurled from a moving car, started out like any other Sunday. My mother woke me up, made me porridge for breakfast. I took my bath while she dressed my baby brother Andrew, who was nine months old. Then we went out to the driveway, but once we were finally all strapped in and ready to go, the car wouldn't start. When the Volkswagen refused to start, inside my head I was praying, Please say we'll just stay home. Please say we'll just stay home. Then I glanced over to see the determined look on my mother's face, her jaw set, and I knew I had a long day ahead of me.

"Come," she said. "We're going to catch minibuses."

My mother and I had a really Tom and Jerry relationship. She was a rigorous disciplinarian, and I was a jerk. She'd send me out to get groceries, and I'd be late because I'd be playing arcade games at the store with the change from the milk and bread. I was a big fan of video games. I was a Street Fighter expert. I could go on and on about a single play. I'd flip a coin in, time would fly by, and the next thing I know, there'd be a woman with a belt behind me. It was a competition. I'd bolt out the door and into Eden Park's dusty streets, clambering over walls and dodging through backyards. It was common in our neighbourhood. Nelson Mandela was released from prison when I was five years old, almost six. I recall seeing it on TV and everyone being overjoyed. I had no idea why we were pleased, only that we were. I was aware that apartheid existed and that it was coming to an end, which was a significant matter, but I didn't comprehend the complexities of it. What I do remember, and what I will never forget, is the ensuing violence. The victory of democracy over apartheid is frequently referred to as the Bloodless Revolution. It's termed so because there was very little white blood spilt. The streets were covered in black blood.

We understood that once the apartheid regime fell, the black man would rule. Which black man was the question? As they jockeyed for dominance, the Inkatha Freedom Party and the ANC, the African National Congress, erupted in bloodshed. The political relationship between these two groups was complex, but the most straightforward way to describe it is as a proxy war between Zulu and Xhosa. The Inkatha was primarily Zulu, violent, and nationalistic. The ANC was a broad alliance of many different tribes, but its leaders were predominantly Xhosa at the time. Instead of working together for peace, they turned on one another, committing atrocities. Riots erupted in large numbers. Hundreds of thousands of people were slaughtered. Necklacing was quite widespread. People would tie someone down and place a rubber tire over his torso, pinning his arms. Then they'd douse him with gasoline, set him ablaze, and burn him alive. Inkatha was victimised by the ANC. The ANC was humiliated by Inkatha. On my way to school one day, I observed one of those burnt bodies on the side of the road. In the evenings, my mother and I would watch the news on our small black-and-white television. Dozens of individuals were slain. Fifty persons have been killed. One hundred persons were slain. That carless Sunday, we did our customary church round, ending at White Church. It was dark and we were alone when we left Rosebank Union. It had been an exhausting day of minibuses from mixed church to black church to white church. It had to be around nine o'clock. You didn't want to be out so late at night back then, with all the violence and rioting. There were no minibuses at the intersection of Jellicoe Avenue and Oxford Road, right in the middle of Johannesburg's rich, white suburbia. The streets were deserted. We waited and waited for the minibus to arrive. The government offered no public transit for blacks during apartheid, but white folks still required us to mop their floors and clean their bathrooms. Because need is the mother of creativity, black people devised their own public transportation system, an informal network of bus routes operated by private associations working fully outside the law. The minibus industry was virtually organised crime because it was absolutely uncontrolled. Different groups took different paths, and they fought over who had control of what. Bribery and overall shadiness were prevalent, as was a large deal of violence and a lot of protection money given to avoid bloodshed. You did not, however, steal a passage from a rival group. Drivers who attempted to steal routes would be killed. Minibuses were unreliable because they were unregulated. They came when they came. They didn't when they didn't have to. I was literally falling asleep on my feet outside Rosebank Union. There isn't a single minibus in sight. My mother eventually suggested, "Let's hitchhike." We walked for what seemed like an eternity until a car pulled up and stopped. We accepted the driver's offer and hopped inside the car. We hadn't gone more than ten feet when a minibus swung directly in front of us, cutting us off. A Zulu driver emerged with an iwisa, a big, traditional Zulu weapon—basically, a war club. They are used to break people's skulls. Another man, a crony, exited the passenger side. They approached the driver's side of the car we were in, grabbed the man who had offered us a ride, dragged him out, and began shoving their clubs in his face. "How come you're stealing our customers?" "Why are you picking up people?"

They appeared to be planning to murder this man. That was something I was aware of happening on occasion. My mother spoke up. "Hey, listen, he was simply trying to help me. Leave him alone. We'll accompany you. That's what we were hoping for in the first place." So we exited the first automobile and boarded the minibus. We were the only people on the minibus. South African minibus drivers are infamous for whining and harassing passengers while they drive, in addition to being violent criminals. This particular driver was enraged. As we drove, he began scolding my mother about being in a car with someone who wasn't her husband. Strange men's lectures did not bother my mother. She ordered him to mind his own business, and when he heard her speak in Xhosa, he became enraged. The preconceptions of Zulu and Xhosa women were as deeply embedded as those of males. Zulu women were polite and dutiful. Xhosa women were disloyal and promiscuous. And here was my mother, his tribal foe, a Xhosa lady alone with two tiny children, one of which was a mixed child. A whore who sleeps with white guys, not just any whore. "Oh, you're a Xhosa," he discovered. "That clarifies things. Climbing into the cars of weird men. "She's a disgusting woman."

He dashed away. He was driving fast and not stopping, just slowing down at junctions to check for traffic before rushing through. He sped down Oxford Road, the lanes empty, no other cars on the road. I was seated closest to the sliding door of the minibus. My mother sat next to me, holding Andrew, my baby. She leaned over to me and whispered, "Trevor, when he slows down at the next intersection, I'm going to open the door and we're going to jump."

I couldn't understand a word she said because I'd passed out by that moment. When we arrived at the next red light, the driver took a moment to look around and check the road. My mother reached over, yanked open the sliding door, grabbed me, and hurled me as far as she could. Then she grabbed Andrew, rolled herself into a ball around him, and leapt out behind me. Until the agony came, it felt like a dream. Bam! I landed hard on the ground. My mother landed next to me, and we tumbled, tumbled, rolled, and rolled. Now I was wide awake. What the hell?! I went from half asleep to shocked. I finally came to a halt and dragged myself up, completely dazed. I looked around and saw my mum standing up. She shouted as she turned to face me.

"Run!"

So I ran, and she ran, and nobody ran as fast as me and my mother. The men jumped out of the minibus and tried to track us down, but they didn't stand a chance. We kept going and going until we arrived at a 24-hour gas station and phoned the cops. The men had long since left.

CHAPTER 2

BORN A CRIME

I grew up in apartheid-era South Africa, which was problematic because I was reared in a mixed family, with me being the mixed child. Patricia Nombuyiselo Noah, my mother, is black. Robert, my father, is white. Swiss/German, to be precise, as Swiss/Germans are invariably. Having sexual intercourse with someone of another race was one of the greatest offences you could commit during apartheid. Needless to say, my parents were the perpetrators of that atrocity. Coloured, black, white, and Indian people were all required by the government to register their race. Millions of people were uprooted and relocated as a result of these classifications. Indian areas were divided from coloured areas, which were separated from black areas, which were all separated from white areas by buffer zones of unoccupied land. Sex between Europeans and natives was prohibited by law, which was later amended to prohibit sex between whites and all nonwhites. The government went to ridiculous lengths to implement these new laws. Breaking them resulted in a five-year prison sentence. My mother will tell you that she never considered the implications of having a mixed child during apartheid. She had a desire to do something, found a way to achieve it, and then did it. She possessed a level of fearlessness that is required to take on something like she did.

If you were a black man during apartheid, you worked on a farm, in a factory, or in a mine. You worked in a factory or as a maid if you were a black woman. Those were really your only options. My mum refused to work in a factory. A black woman learning to type was like a blind person learning to drive at the time. It's a commendable effort, but you're unlikely to be called upon to carry out the assignment. White-collar and skilled-labour employment were legally reserved for whites. Black individuals were not employed in offices. My mother, on the other hand, was a rebel, and fortunately for her, her disobedience came at the right time.

In the early 1980s, the South African government began implementing minimal reforms in an attempt to assuage worldwide outrage over apartheid's horrors and human rights violations. One of these improvements was the limited hiring of black people in low-level white-collar occupations. Typists are an example. She found a position as a secretary at ICI, a global pharmaceutical business in Braamfontein, a Johannesburg suburb, through an employment agency. You need a pass with your ID number to leave the township for work in the city or for any other reason; otherwise, you may be arrested. There was also a curfew: blacks had to be back home in the township by a particular hour or face incarceration. My mum was unconcerned. She was determined never to return home. So she lingered in town, hiding and sleeping in public facilities until she learnt the city's laws from the other black women who had managed to live there: prostitutes.

Many of the town's prostitutes were Xhosa. They spoke my mother's language and taught her survival skills. They showed her how to disguise herself in a pair of maid's overalls in order to walk around the city without being stopped. They also introduced her to white men looking to rent out apartments in town. Many of these guys were foreigners, Germans and Portuguese, who didn't care about the law and were willing to sign a lease that provided a home for a prostitute to live and work in exchange for a constant piece on the side. My mother was not interested in such an arrangement, but thanks to her job, she was able to pay her rent. She met a German man through one of her prostitute pals, and he agreed to let her live in his apartment. She moved in and purchased a slew of maid's overalls to wear. She was arrested several times for not having her ID on the way home from work and for being in a white zone after hours. For violating the pass laws, the penalty was thirty days in jail or a fine of fifty rand, about half her monthly earnings. She'd pull together the cash, pay the fine, and go about her business. My mom's secret flat was in a neighbourhood called Hillbrow. She lived in number 203. Down the corridor was a tall, brown-haired, brown-eyed Swiss/German expat named Robert. He lived in 206. Living alone in the city, not being trusted and not being able to trust, my mother started spending more and more time in the company of someone with whom she felt safe: the tall Swiss man down the corridor in 206. He was forty-six. She was twenty-four. He was quiet and reserved; she was wild and free. She would stop by his flat to chat; they'd go to underground get-togethers, go dancing at the nightclub with the rotating dance floor. Something clicked. I know that there was a genuine bond and a love between my parents. I saw it. But how romantic their relationship was, to what extent they were just friends, I can't say. These are things a child doesn't ask. All I do know is that one day she made her proposal.

"I want to have a kid," she told him.

"I don't want kids," he said.

"I didn't ask you to have a kid. I asked you to help me to have my kid. I just want the sperm from you."

"I'm Catholic," he said. "We don't do such things."

"You do know," she replied, "that I could sleep with you and go away and you would never know if you had a child or not. But I don't want that. Honour me with your eyes so that I can live peacefully. I want a child of my own, and I want it from you. You will be able to see it as much as you like, but you will have no obligations. You don't have to talk about it. You don't have to pay for it. Just make this child for me." For my father's part, I know that for a long time he kept saying no. Eventually he said yes. Why he said yes is a question I will never have the answer to. Nine months after that, on February 20, 1984, my mother checked into Hillbrow Hospital for a scheduled C-section delivery. Estranged from her family, pregnant by a man she could not be seen with in public, she was alone. The doctors took her up to the delivery room, cut open her belly, and reached in and pulled out a half-white, half-black child who violated any number of laws, statutes, and regulations—I was born a crime.

My father's name does not appear on my birth certificate. Officially, he was never my father. And, true to her promise, my mother was prepared for him not to be involved. She'd rented a new apartment in Joubert Park, a neighbourhood near Hillbrow, and that's where she took me when she got out of the hospital. The following week, she went to see him without the baby. To her amazement, he inquired as to where she was. "You stated that you didn't want to be involved," she continued. And he hadn't, but once I was here, he realised he couldn't have a son living nearby and not be a part of my life. So, as much as our unusual situation allowed, the three of us became a kind of family. My mother was my landlord. We'd sneak around to see my father whenever we could.

CHAPTER 3

CHAMELEON

I was playing with my cousins one afternoon. They were my patients, and I was a doctor. I was using a set of matches to operate on my cousin Bulelwa's ear when I accidentally ruptured her eardrum. Everything went to hell. My grandmother rushed in from the kitchen. "Kwenzeka ntoni?!" "What's going on?" My cousin's head was filled with blood. We were all in tears. Bulelwa's ear was sewn up and the bleeding was stopped by my granny. But we didn't stop sobbing. Because we'd clearly done something we weren't supposed to do, and we knew we'd be punished. My grandmother finished with Bulelwa's ear and whipped out a belt, beating the s*** out of him. Then she beat the crap out of Mlungisi as well. She never touched me.

My mother returned home from work later that night. She discovered my cousin with an ear bandage and my grandmother crying at the kitchen table.

"What's going on?" my mother said.

"Oh, Nombuyiselo," she commented. "Trevor is such a jerk. He's the most mischievous boy I've ever met in my life."

"Then you should hit him."

"I'm afraid I can't hit him."

"Why not?" says one.

"Because I don't know how to strike a white child," she explained. "I understand a black youngster. You strike a black child, and they remain black. When you hit Trevor, he goes blue, green, yellow, and red. Those are colours I've never seen before. I'm afraid I'm going to snap him. I do not want to murder a white person. I'm terrified. I'm not going near him." That she never did.

My grandmother treated me as though I were white. My grandfather did the same, but he was even more extreme. He addressed me as "Mastah." He persisted in driving me as if he were my chauffeur in the car. "Mastah must always sit in the backseat." I never pressed him on it. What did I intend to say? "I believe your perception of race is flawed, Grandfather." No. I was five years old. I took a seat near the back. I can't even begin to list the benefits of being "white" in a black family. I was having a fantastic time. My own family essentially performed what the American judicial system does: I was treated better than the black kids. I was given a warning and allowed off for misbehaviour that my relatives would have been punished for. And I was far more deviant than either of my cousins. It didn't even come close. It was my fault if something broke or someone stole Granny's cookies. I was a nuisance. My mother was the only person I genuinely dreaded. She was of the opinion that if you spare the rod, you pamper the child. Everyone else responded, "No, he's different," and they let me off the hook. Growing up the way I did, I saw how simple it is for white people to become comfortable with a system that gives them everything. I knew my cousins were being punished for things I'd done, but I didn't want to change my grandmother's mind since that would mean I'd be beaten as well. Why would I do such a thing? So I could feel better? Being beaten made me feel even worse. I had a decision to make. I could advocate for racial justice at home, or I could eat granny's cookies. I choose the cookies.

"Indoda yomlungu!" the kids on the street would yell whenever they spotted me. "The white man!" exclaims the narrator. Some of them would flee. Others would summon their parents to come look at them. Others would approach me and try to touch me to check if I was genuine. It was complete chaos. What I didn't realise at the time was that the other youngsters had no idea what a white person was. The township's black children did not flee. There were few televisions in use.

As a child, I recognized that humans came in many hues, but in my mind, white, black, and brown were all different kinds of chocolate. Dad represented white chocolate, Mom represented dark chocolate, and I represented milk chocolate. But we were all made of chocolate. I had no idea it had anything to do with "race." I had no idea what race was. My mother never described my father as white or myself as mixed. So when the other kids in Soweto labelled me "white," despite the fact that I was light brown, I assumed they had their colours jumbled up and hadn't learnt them properly. My mother made certain that English was the first language I learned. Speaking English is the one thing that can offer you an advantage if you are black in South Africa. English is the money language. English comprehension is used to measure intellect. If you're seeking for work, English can mean the difference between getting hired and staying unemployed. If you're in court, knowing English can be the difference between a fine and a prison sentence. As a young man, one day I was strolling down the street when I noticed a bunch of Zulus closing in on me, and I could hear them discussing how they were going to mug me. "Asibambe yomlungu autie. "Ngemuva kwakhe ngapha mina ngizo qhamuka ngemuva kwakhe." "Let's go find this white guy." I'll come up behind him if you move to his left." I had no idea what to do. I couldn't escape, so I wheeled around and asked, "Kodwa bafwethu yingani singavele sibambe umuntu inkunzi?" Senzeni. My name is Mina ngikulindele." "Why don't we just mug someone together, guys?" I'm prepared. Let's get started."

They looked stunned for a while, then burst out laughing. "I'm so sorry, guy. We mistook you for someone else. We weren't attempting to steal anything from you. We were attempting to rob white individuals. "Have a nice day, man." They were ready to kill me until they realised we belonged to the same tribe, and then we were cool. That, and many other minor instances throughout my life, taught me that language, more than colour, determines who you are to others. I became a chameleon. My colour did not change, but I could alter your perception of it. If you spoke to me in Zulu, I would respond in Zulu. I replied in Tswana if you spoke to me in Tswana. I may not have looked like you, but if I spoke like you, I was you. As apartheid ended, South Africa's best private schools began to accept pupils of all races. My mother's company provided bursaries and scholarships to low-income families, and she was able to get me into Maryvale College, a prestigious private Catholic school. Nuns teach classes. On Fridays, there is a mass. The entire thing. I started preschool when I was three years old and primary school when I was five. We had a diverse group of students in my class. There are black children, white children, Indian children, and coloured children. The majority of the white kids were well-off. Almost every child of colour was not. However, due to scholarships, we all sat at the same table. We all dressed in identical maroon blazers, grey trousers, and skirts. We were both reading the same books. Our teachers were the same. There was no racial division. Every clique was multiracial. Kids were still taunted and bullied, but it was for the typical reasons: being big or skinny, tall or short, smart or dumb. I don't recall anyone being teased because of their race. I didn't learn to set boundaries for what I was supposed to enjoy or dislike. I had the freedom to explore myself. I had a thing for white girls. I had a thing for black girls. Nobody ever asked me who I was. Trevor was my name.

CHAPTER 4

LOOPHOLES

"I chose to have you because I wanted something to love and something that would love me unconditionally in return—and then I gave birth to the most selfish piece of shit on the planet, and all it ever did was cry and eat and shit and say, 'Me, me, me, me me,'" my mother used to say. My mother expected having a kid to be like having a lover, but every child is born the centre of its own universe, incapable of knowing the world outside its own wants and requirements, and I was no exception. I was a voracious reader as a child. I devoured cartons of books and desired more, more, more. I ate like a pig. I should have been obese if I had eaten like that. At one time, my family assumed I had worms. Whenever I went to my cousins' house for the holidays, my mother would leave me off with a bag of tomatoes, onions, and potatoes, as well as a large sack of cornmeal. That was her approach to preventing any complaints about my visit. My grandmother always gave me seconds, which none of the other kids got. My grandmother would hand me the pot and say, "Finish it." You contacted Trevor if you didn't want to wash the dishes. They referred to me as the family's garbage can. I ate and ate and ate.

I, too, was hyperactive. I craved continual stimulation and activity. When I was a toddler, if you didn't hold my arm in a death grasp, I was off, running full-speed toward the road. I enjoyed being chased. I thought it was a game. The ancient grannies my mother hired to look after me while she was at work? I'd leave them in tears. They'd be crying when my mother came home. My excess energy would find its way into general naughtiness and misbehaviour if it wasn't expended. I considered myself to be the greatest prankster. During class, every teacher used overhead projectors to project their notes onto the wall. One day, I went around and removed the magnifying lens from every projector in every classroom. Another time, I emptied a fire extinguisher into the school piano since I knew we were going to have a performance at assembly the next day. The pianist sat down and played the first note, and all this froth exploded out of the piano.

Fire and knives were my two favourite things. They were endlessly fascinating to me. Knives were cool. I got them from pawnshops and garage sales: flick knives, butterfly knives, the Rambo knife, and the Crocodile Dundee knife. But fire was the final. I was fascinated with fire, especially fireworks. Every year on November 5th, my mother would purchase us a ton of pyrotechnics, like a mini-arsenal. I realised I could take the gunpowder from all of the pyrotechnics and make my own enormous firework. One afternoon, while playing with my cousin and filling an empty plant pot with a massive mound of explosives, I was sidetracked by some Black Cat firecrackers. Instead of lighting it to make it explode, you could break it in two and light it to turn it into a mini-flamethrower. I stopped mid-build to play with the Black Cats and accidentally dropped a match into the pile. The entire thing erupted, hurling a big ball of flame at my face. Mlungisi yelled, and my mother dashed into the yard in a panic. "What happened?!"

I played it cool, even though I could still feel the heat of the fireball on my face. "Oh, nothing. Nothing happened."

"Were you playing with fire?!"

"No."

She shook her head. "You know what? I would beat you, but Jesus has already exposed your lies."

"Huh?"

"Go to the bathroom and look at yourself."

I went to the toilet and looked in the mirror. My eyebrows were gone and the front inch or so of my hair was completely burned off.

From an adult's point of view, I was destructive and out of control, but as a child I didn't think of it that way. I never wanted to destroy. I wanted to create. I wasn't burning my eyebrows. I was creating fire. I wasn't breaking overhead projectors. I was creating chaos, to see how people reacted. And I couldn't help it. There's a condition kids suffer from, a compulsive disorder that makes them do things they themselves don't understand. You can tell a child, "Whatever you do, don't draw on the wall. You can draw on this paper. You can draw in this book. You can draw on any surface you want. But do not draw or write or colour on the wall." The child will look you dead in the eye and say, "Got it." Ten minutes later the child is drawing on the wall. You start screaming. "Why the hell are you drawing on the wall?!" The child looks at you, and he genuinely has no idea why he drew on the wall. As a kid, I remember having that feeling all the time. Every time I got punished, as my mom was whooping my ass, I'd be thinking, Why did I just do that? I knew not to do that. She told me not to do that. Then once the hiding was over I'd say to myself, I'm going to be so good from here on. I'm never ever going to do a bad thing in my life ever ever ever ever ever—and to remember not to do anything bad, let me write something on the wall to remind myself...and then I would pick up a crayon and get straight back into it, and I never understood why.

My connection with my mother was similar to that of a cop and a criminal in a movie—the dogged investigator and the crafty mastermind she's driven to apprehend. They're bitter rivals, but damn, they respect one another and, somehow, they grow to enjoy each other. My mother would occasionally catch up to me, but she was always one step behind and constantly gave me the side look. One day, a youngster. I'm going to catch you someday and lock you up for the rest of your life. Then I'd reciprocate with a nod. Have a pleasant evening, Officer. That was the story of my entire upbringing. She changed tactics since I was too savvy to be misled by the time I was seven or eight. Our lives had devolved into a courtroom drama, with two lawyers continually disputing technicalities and loopholes. My mother was intelligent and had a keen tongue, but I was faster in an argument. She'd become agitated because she couldn't keep up. So she began writing me letters. That way, she could make her arguments without having to engage in verbal fighting. If I had duties to do, I'd arrive home to find an envelope, possibly from the landlord, placed under the door. I'd deliver the letter to her and stand there while she read it. She'd always tear it up and toss it in the trash. "Rubbish! This is nonsense!" Then she'd start launching herself at me, and I'd cry, "Ah-ah-ah. No. You must compose a letter." I'd then walk to my room and wait for her response. This might go on for days at a time. The letter was written to settle small disagreements. My mother used the asswhooping method for serious transgressions. My mother, like other black South African mothers, was a strict disciplinarian. She'd reach for the belt or switch if I pushed her too far. That was the way it was back then. Almost all of my pals experienced the same problem. When it came to discipline, Catholic school was no joke. Whenever I got into trouble with the nuns at Maryvale they'd rap me on the knuckles with the edge of a metal ruler. For cursing they'd wash my mouth out with soap. For serious offences I'd get sent to the principal's office. Only the principal could give you an official hiding. You'd have to bend over and he'd hit your ass with this flat rubber thing, like the sole of a shoe. Whenever the principal would hit me, it was like he was afraid to do it too hard. One day I was hiding and I thought, Man, if only my mom hit me like this, " I started laughing. I couldn't help it. The principal was quite disturbed. "If you're laughing while you're getting beaten," he said, "then something is definitely wrong with you."

That was the first of three times the school made my mom take me to a psychologist to be evaluated. Every psychologist who examined me came back and said, "There's nothing wrong with this kid." I wasn't ADD. I wasn't a sociopath. I was just creative and independent and full of energy. The therapists did give me a series of tests, and they came to the conclusion that I was either going to make an excellent criminal or be very good at catching criminals, because I could always find loopholes in the law. Whenever I thought a rule wasn't logical, I'd find my way around it. For that, I got another hiding and a second visit to the psychologist. The third and last visit to the shrink occurred in sixth grade. A child was harassing me. He threatened to beat me up, so I brought one of my knives to school. I didn't intend to use it; I simply wanted to have it. The school was unconcerned. That was their final straw. I wasn't precisely expelled. "Trevor, we can expel you," the principal stated as he sat me down. You should seriously consider if you want to return to Maryvale next year." He probably thought he was issuing an ultimatum to get me to change my ways. But I felt like he was giving me a way out, so I took it. "No," I replied. "I don't want to be here." And with that, Catholic school came to an end. Surprisingly, I did not get into trouble with my mother when this occurred. At home, there was no ass-whooping waiting for me. She'd lost her bursary when she quit her work at ICI, and paying for private school was becoming a financial burden. But she also thought the school was overreacting. In reality, she probably sided with me against Maryvale more often than not. She completely agreed with me on the Eucharist. "Let me get this straight," she explained to the principal. "You're punishing a child because he desires Jesus' body and blood?" Why shouldn't he be able to have those things? He should have them, of course." She also told the school that making me see a therapist for laughing while the principal slapped me was ludicrous.

My mother had been dating her new lover, Abel, for about a year when I was seven years old, but I was too young to realise who they were to one another. It was simply "Hey, that's mom's friend who's always around." Abel was a great guy, and I liked him. Back then, if you were a black person looking to reside in the suburbs, you had to find a white family renting out their servants' quarters or perhaps their garage, which was what Abel had done. He resided in Orange Grove in a white family's garage, which he'd converted into a cottage-style thing with a hot plate and a bed. He'd come and sleep at our house on occasion, and we'd go stay with him on other occasions. Staying in a garage when we owned our own home wasn't ideal, but Orange Grove was close to my school and my mother's place of employment, so it had its advantages. This white family also had a black maid who lived in the servants' quarters in the garden, and whenever we went there, I'd play with her son. My passion for fire was in full flower at the time. Everyone was at work one afternoon—my mother, Abel, and both white parents—and the child and I were playing together while his mother was cleaning the house. At the time, I enjoyed using a magnifying glass to burn my name into pieces of wood. You had to aim the lens and get the focus just perfect before getting the flame and moving it gently to burn forms, letters, and patterns. It piqued my interest.

I was showing this youngster how to do it that afternoon. We were inside the servants' quarters, which had been extended to the back of the house and were full with wooden ladders, buckets of old paint, and turpentine. I also had a box of matches and all of my standard fire-starting supplies with me. We sat on an old mattress that they used to sleep on the floor, which was just a sack filled with dried straw. The light was shining through the window as I demonstrated how to burn his name into a piece of plywood. We took a pause to have a snack at one point. I placed the magnifying glass and matches on the mattress before we left. When we returned a few minutes later, we discovered the shed had one of those self-locking doors from the inside. We couldn't get back in without first going to get his mother, so we opted to play in the yard. After a while, I observed smoke seeping out of the window frame cracks. I dashed over and peered inside. In the middle of the straw mattress, where we'd left the matches and the magnifying glass, a small fire was burning. We dashed out the door and summoned the maid. She arrived, but she had no idea what to do. The door was locked, and before we could find out how to get into the shed, everything became stuck—the mattress, ladders, paint, turpentine, everything. The flames were moving swiftly. The roof quickly caught fire, and the blaze moved to the main house, where it burned and burned and burned. Smoke billowed into the heavens. The fire department had been contacted by a neighbour, and the sirens were on their way. We raced out to the road with this youngster and the maid and watched as the firemen tried to put it out, but it was too late. Nothing remained but a burnt brick-and-mortar shell, the roof gone and the interior destroyed. The white family returned home and stood on the street, staring at their house's ruins. They questioned the maid what had happened, and she asked her son, who completely snitched. "Trevor had some matches," he explained. Nothing was spoken to me by the family. They didn't seem to know what to say. They were extremely perplexed. They didn't call the cops or threaten to sue. Was it their intention to arrest a seven-year-old for arson? And we were so impoverished that you couldn't even sue us. They also had insurance, so that was the end of the matter. They kicked Abel out of the garage, which I thought was amusing because the garage was the only piece of property that had not been destroyed. I saw no reason for Abel to depart, yet they forced him to. We collected his belongings, loaded them into our car, and went back to Eden Park; Abel basically lived with us from then on. He and my mother got into a heated argument. "Your son has burned down my life!" But there was no penalty for me on that particular day. My mother was in too much shock. There's being wicked and then burning down a white person's house. She was at a loss for what to do. I didn't feel horrible about it in the least. I still don't know. The lawyer in me believes I am absolutely innocent. There were matches, a magnifying glass, a mattress, and then, apparently, a series of horrible happenings. Sometimes things catch fire. That is why there is a fire department. Everyone in my family, however, will tell you that "Trevor burned down a house." If folks thought I was bad before the fire, I was notorious afterward. One of my uncles stopped referring to me as Trevor. He referred to me as "Terror" instead. "Don't leave that kid alone in your home," he'd warn. "He'll burn it to the ground." My cousin Mlungisi still doesn't understand how I survived being as naughty as I was for as long as I did, or how I survived the number of hidings I received. Why did I continue to misbehave? How did I ever forget my lesson? My cousins were both excellent students. Mlungisi may have one in his life. After that, he claimed he never wanted to go through anything like that again, and he always followed the rules from then on. But another feature I inherited from my mother was her capacity to forget the hardship of life. I recall the event that created the trauma, but I do not dwell on it. I never let a painful memory keep me from attempting something new. If you dwell on the asskicking you got from your mother or the asskicking you got from life, you'll stop pushing the boundaries and breaking the rules. It's best to accept it, mourn for a while, then wake up the next day and move on. You'll have a few bruises to remember you of what happened, which is OK. But the bruises fade after a while, and they fade for a reason: it's time to get up to some crap again.

CHAPTER 5

THE MULBERRY TREE

At the end of our street in Eden Park, right in a bend at the top of the road, stood a giant mulberry tree growing out of someone's front yard. Every year when it bore fruit the neighbourhood kids would go and pick berries from it, eating as many as they could and filling up bags to take home. They would all play under the tree together. I had to play under the tree by myself. I didn't have any friends in Eden Park. The animosity I felt from the coloured people I encountered growing up was one of the hardest things I've ever had to deal with. It taught me that it is easier to be an insider as an outsider than to be an outsider as an insider. If a white guy chooses to immerse himself in hip-hop culture and only hang out with black people, black people will say, "Cool, white guy. Do what you need to do." If a black guy chooses to button up his blackness to live among white people and play lots of golf, white people will say, "Fine. I like Brian. He's safe." But try being a black person who immerses himself in white culture while still living in the black community. Try being a white person who adopts the trappings of black culture while still living in the white community. You will face more hate and ridicule and ostracism than you can even begin to fathom. People are willing to accept you if they see you as an outsider trying to assimilate into their world. But when they see you as a fellow tribe member attempting to disavow the tribe, that is something they will never forgive. That is what happened to me in Eden Park.

During apartheid, a white person was defined as "one who in appearance is obviously a white person and is generally not accepted as a coloured person; or is generally accepted as a white person and is not in appearance obviously a white person." In other words, it was utterly random. This is where the government devised items like the pencil test. The pencil went into your hair if you were applying to be white. You were white if it fell out. You were coloured if it stayed inside. You were exactly who the government claimed you were.

Sometimes it came down to a lone cashier looking you in the eyes and making a hasty choice. He could tick whatever box made sense to him, selecting where you could live, who you could marry, what employment you could have, and what rights and benefits you could have based on how high your cheekbones were or how big your nose was.

And it wasn't only that people of colour were promoted to white. Sometimes persons of colour were mistaken for Indians. Indians were occasionally coloured. Blacks were sometimes promoted to coloured, and coloureds were sometimes relegated to black. Of course, whites may also be downgraded to coloured. That was crucial. Those mixed lineages were constantly lurking, waiting to break through, and white people's fear of losing their standing kept them in line. If two white parents had a child and the government determined the child was too dark, even if both parents supplied documents proving their whiteness, the infant may be categorised as coloured, and the family would have to make a decision. Do they give up their whiteness to live as coloured people in a coloured neighbourhood? Or would they split up, with the mother taking the coloured child to live in the ghetto and the father staying white to support them?

Many black people lived in this limbo, a true purgatory, eternally pining for the white fathers who had abandoned them, and as a result, they could be extremely racist to one another. Boesman was the most commonly used coloured slur. "Bushman." "Bushie." Because it emphasised their blackness, their primitivism. The worst way to disrespect a person of colour was to imply that they were black in some way. One of the most pernicious aspects of apartheid was that it educated coloured people that it was black people who held them back. Apartheid said that the main reason coloured people couldn't have first-class status was that black people might utilise their colour to get past the gates and enjoy the privileges of whites.

That's exactly what apartheid did: it convinced every group that their exclusion was due to the other race. It's essentially the doorman saying, "We can't let you in because of your friend Darren and his ugly shoes." "Screw you, Black Darren," you say to Darren. You're stifling my progress." The bouncer then responds to Darren, "No, it's actually your friend Sizwe and his weird hair." So Darren says, "Screw you, Sizwe," and everyone now despises everyone else. But the truth is that none of you were ever going to be admitted to that club.

So you can imagine how weird it was for me. I was mixed but not coloured—coloured by complexion but not by culture. Because of that I was seen as a coloured person who didn't want to be coloured.

CHAPTER 6

OUTSIDER

I started grade eight at Sandringham High School after graduating primary school at H. A. Jack. Even after apartheid, most black people continued to live in townships and territories originally designated as homelands, where the only government schools available were the shattered ruins of the Bantu system. There are no cafeterias in South African schools. At Sandringham, we'd buy our lunch at the tuck shop, a small canteen, and then eat wherever we pleased on the school grounds—the quad, the courtyard, the playground, whatever. Children would separate and form cliques and groupings. In most cases, people were still organised by colour, but you could see how they all blended and darkened into one another. The majority of the soccer players were black children. Tennis players were predominantly white children. The kids that played cricket were a diverse group. The Chinese kids would congregate near the prefabricated structures. The matrics, or seniors in South Africa, would congregate on the quad. Popular, gorgeous girls would congregate here, while computer geeks would congregate there. The racial groups were formed as a result of how race intersected with class and location in the real world. Suburban youngsters socialised with other suburban kids. Township kids socialised with other Township kids. Thanks to my long walk to school, I was late every single day. I'd have to stop off in the prefect's office to write my name down for detention. I was the patron saint of detention. Already late, I'd run to join my morning classes—maths, English, biology, whatever. The last period before break was assembly. The pupils would come together in the assembly hall, each grade seated row by row, and the teachers and the prefects would get up onstage and go over the business of what was happening in the school—announcements, awards, that sort of thing. The names of the kids with detention were announced at every assembly, and I was always one of them. Always. Every single day. It was a running joke. The perfect would say, "Detentions for today..." and I would stand up automatically. It was like the Oscars and I was Meryl Streep. There was one time I stood up and then the prefect named the five people and I wasn't one of them. Everyone burst out laughing. Somebody yelled out, "Where's Trevor?!" The perfect man looked at the paper and shook his head. "Nope." The entire hall erupted with cheers and applause. "Yay!!!!"

Then, immediately after assembly, there would be a race to the tuck shop because the queue to buy food was so long. Every minute you spent in the queue was working against your break time. The sooner you got your food, the longer you had to eat, play a game of soccer, or hang out. Also, if you got there late, the best food was gone. Two things were true about me at that age. One, I was still the fastest kid in school. And two, I had no pride. The second we were dismissed from assembly I would run like a bat out of hell to the tuck shop so I could be the first one there. I was always first in line. I became notorious for being that guy, so much so that people started coming up to me in line. "Hey, can you buy this for me?" Which would piss off the kids behind me because it was basically cutting the line. So people started approaching me during assembly. They'd say, "Hey, I've got ten rand. If you buy my food for me, I'll give you two." That's when I learned: time is money. I realised people would pay me to buy their food because I was willing to run for it. I started telling everyone at the assembly, "Place your orders. Give me a list of what you want, give me a percentage of what you're going to spend, and I'll buy your food for you."

I became famous overnight. My most frequent customers were overweight men. They loved food but were unable to run. "This is fantastic!" said all these affluent, obese white youngsters. My folks lavish me, I have money, and now I have a method to acquire meals without having to work for it—while still getting my break." I had so many customers that I had to turn away children. I had a rule: I would only accept five orders per day from high bidders. I'd make enough money to purchase my lunch with other kids' money and keep the lunch money my mother gave me for pocket money. Then I could take the bus instead of walking home or save up for whatever I wanted. Every day, I'd take orders, assembly would end, and I'd run out the door to get everyone's hot dogs, Cokes, and muffins. You could even tell me where you'd be and I'd deliver it to you if you paid me extra. I'd found my calling. I learnt to glide fluidly between groups because I belonged to none. I was afloat. I was and still am a cultural chameleon. I discovered how to blend. I could participate in sports with the jocks. I could converse with the nerds about computers. I could join the township youngsters in a circle dance. I went from person to person, working, conversing, telling jokes, and delivering deliveries. I was similar to a weed dealer, but for food. The cannabis man is always welcome at parties. He is not a member of the circle, but he has been invited to join it temporarily because of what he can provide. That was my personality. Always an outcast. As an outsider, you have the option of withdrawing into a shell, remaining anonymous and invisible. You can also go the opposite route. By opening out, you defend yourself. You don't want to be accepted for everything you are; you only want to be accepted for the part of yourself that you're prepared to share. It was humour for me. I discovered that even if I didn't belong to any particular group, I could be a part of any group that was laughing. I'd pop by, pass out refreshments, and crack a few jokes. I'd put up a show for them. I'd listen in on their chat, learn more about their organisation, and then depart. I never remained longer than I had to. I wasn't well-liked, but I wasn't an outcast either. I was everywhere with everyone and nowhere by myself at the same time.

CHAPTER 7

GO HITLER!

Bolo, Bruce Lee, and John were three Chinese students who transferred to Sandringham when I was in ninth school. Out of a thousand students, they were the only Chinese students. Bolo received his moniker because he resembled Bolo Yeung from the Jean-Claude Van Damme film Bloodsport. Bruce Lee's name was indeed Bruce Lee, which made our lives easier. Bruce Lee was a Chinese man who was quiet, good-looking, and in terrific form. This is magic, we thought. Thank you for delivering us Bruce Lee, Jesus. John was just John, which was odd given the other two. Bolo was one of my tuck-shop customers, so I got to know him. Bolo's father and mother were both accomplished pirates. They sold pirated video games at flea markets. Bolo, the son of pirates, did the same—he began selling bootleg PlayStation games around school. Kids would hand over their PlayStations to him, and he'd return them a few days later with a chip that allowed them to play unlicensed games, which he'd then sell. Bolo was buddies with Andrew, a Caucasian child and fellow pirate who dealt in bootleg CDs. Andrew was two classes above me and a true computer geek; he even had a CD writer at home when no one else had.

I overheard Andrew and Bolo grumbling about the black students at school one day while doing my tuck-shop rounds. They'd figured out that they could take Andrew and Bolo's products, say "I'll pay you later," and then not pay since Andrew and Bolo were too afraid of black people to go back and ask for the money. "Listen, you shouldn't get upset," I added as I leaned in on their chat. Because black people don't have much money, we want to get more things for less money. But allow me to assist you. I'll act as your go-between. You give me the item, and I'll sell it and collect the proceeds. In exchange, you give me a percentage of the sale." They immediately liked the concept, and we became partners. I was properly placed as the tuck-shop guy. I had already set up my network. I only had to tap into it. I was able to save up enough money from selling CDs and videogames to upgrade my own computer with new components and extra memory. Andrew, the computer expert, demonstrated how to do it, where to get the cheapest parts, how to build and repair them. He also demonstrated how his company operated, including how to download music and where to obtain rewritable CDs in quantity. The only item I didn't have was my own CD writer, which was the most expensive component. A CD writer cost about 2,000 rand at the time, the same as the rest of the computer. For a year, I served as a go-between for Bolo and Andrew. Then Bolo dropped out of school; the word was that his parents were arrested. I worked for Andrew from then on, until he decided to leave the game just as he was ready to matriculate. "Trevor," he said, "you've been a loyal partner." As a token of gratitude, he left me his CD writer. Let's start with the fact that black people had little access to computers at the time. But a CD burner? That was legendary stuff. It was legendary. Andrew transformed my life the day he handed it to me. Because of him, I now had complete control over manufacturing, sales, and distribution—everything I needed to secure the bootleg company.

I considered myself a natural capitalist. I enjoyed selling things, and I was selling something that everyone wanted but no one else could supply. I sold my discs for 30 rand (about $3). A standard CD in the store costs between 100 and 150 rand. People who started buying from me said they would never buy real CDs again because the price was too fantastic. I had a natural business sense, but I knew nothing about music at the time, which was unusual for someone running a music-piracy firm. The only music I knew was Christian music from church, which was also the only music allowed in my mother's house. Andrew got me a 1x CD writer, which meant it copied at the same speed as it played. Every day, I'd leave school, go to my room, and copy CDs for five to six hours. I made my own surround-sound system out of old automobile speakers I salvaged from Abel's junkers and hung them about the room. Even though I had to wait there while each CD played, I didn't listen to them for a long time. I knew it was against dealer policy to get high on your own supply. I could get anything from anyone thanks to the Internet. I never evaluated other people's musical tastes. I got you the new Nirvana because you wanted it. You wanted the new DMX, so I got it for you. Local South African music was popular, but black American music, particularly hip-hop and R&B, was in high demand. Jagged Edge was massive. The number 112 was enormous. I sold a lot of Montell Jordan merchandise. Montell Jordan is everywhere. I began with a dial-up connection and a 24k modem. An album would take a day to download. But technology progressed, and I continued to reinvest in the company. I switched to a 56k modem. I purchased speedier CD writers as well as several CD writers. I began downloading, copying, and selling more. That's when I recruited my own middlemen, my friend Tom from Northview and my pal Bongani from Alex.

"You know what would make a lot of money?" Bongani said to me one day. Instead of copying entire albums, why not compile the finest tracks from many albums onto a single CD, because consumers simply want to hear the songs they like?" That sounded like a fantastic idea, so I began creating mix CDs. Those were a big hit. "Can you make the tracks fade into one another so the music moves from track one to track two without a break and the beat continues?" Bongani asked a few weeks later. It'll be like a DJ performing a full set all night." That sounded like a fantastic concept as well. I downloaded an application called BPM, which stands for "beats per minute." It had a graphical interface that looked like two vinyl records stacked on top of one another, and I could mix and fade between songs, virtually anything a DJ can do live. I started manufacturing party CDs, which sold like hotcakes as well. The economy was thriving. By matric, I was making 500 rand each week. To put it in context, maids in South Africa still make less than that today. If you're trying to support a family, it's a pittance, but as a sixteen-year-old living at home with no real expenses, I was living the dream. I had money for the first time in my life, and it was the most liberating feeling in the world. The first thing I discovered about money was that it provided me with options. People do not wish to be wealthy. They want the ability to choose. The more money you have, the more options you have. That is financial liberty.

With money, I had a whole new level of freedom: I went to McDonald's. People in America don't understand why, yet when an American business opens a location in a third-world country, people go insane. That is still true today. Last year, the first Burger King debuted in South Africa, and there was a line around the block. It was a big deal. "I have to eat at Burger King," everyone was saying. Have you seen it? It's from the United States." The amusing thing was that the queue was entirely composed of white folks. White people went insane for Burger King. Whatever, black people said. Burger King was unnecessary for black folks. Our hearts belonged to KFC and McDonald's. The strange thing about McDonald's is that we heard about it long before it arrived, most likely through movies. We never imagined having one in South Africa; McDonald's appeared like one of those uniquely American things that can't be found anyplace else. We thought we'd adore McDonald's even before we tried it, and we did. South Africa used to open more McDonald's than any other country in the world. Mandela brought freedom, and freedom brought McDonald's. Not long after we moved to Highlands North, a McDonald's opened just two blocks away, but my mother would never pay for us to dine there. I said, "Let's do this with my own money." I put everything on the line. There was no such thing as "supersize" at the time; "large" was the largest. So I strolled up to the counter, feeling very proud of myself, and placed my money on the counter, saying, "I'll have a large number one."

McDonald's captured my heart. McDonald's tasted like America to me. McDonald's represents America. You see it promoted and it appears to be fantastic. You want it. You purchase it. You take your first bite, and it takes your breath away. It's even greater than you could have anticipated. Then, halfway through, you discover that's not all that it seems. After a few bites, you realise, "Hmm, there's a lot wrong with this." Then you're done, you miss it terribly, and you return for more. I never ate at home again after experiencing America. I ate only at McDonald's. McDonald's, McDonald's, McDonald's, McDonald's, McDonald's. My mother would try to cook me dinner every night.

"Tonight, we're having chicken livers."

"No, I'm having McDonald's."

"Tonight, we're having dog bones."

"I believe I'll go with McDonald's again."

"Tonight, we're having chicken feet."

"Hmmmmm…Okay, I'll take part. But I'm going to McDonald's tomorrow."

The money continued coming in, and I was having a great time. I was so cocky that I got a cordless phone. This was before the widespread use of cellphones. The range on this cordless phone was good enough that I could leave the base outside my window, go two blocks to McDonald's, order my large number one, walk back home, go up to my room, and turn on my computer while talking. I was the guy going down the street, holding a massive phone to my ear with the aerial fully extended, talking to a friend. "Yeah, I'm just going to McDonald's…"

Life was good, and none of it would have happened without Andrew. Without him, I would never have mastered the world of music piracy and lived a life of endless McDonald's. What he did, on a small scale, showed me how important it is to empower the dispossessed and the disenfranchised in the wake of oppression. Andrew was white. His family had access to education, resources, and computers. For generations, while his people were preparing to go to university, my people were crowded into thatched huts singing, "Two times two is four. Three times two is six. La la la la la." My family had been denied the things his family had taken for granted. I had a natural talent for selling to people, but without knowledge and resources, where was that going to get me? People always lecture the poor: "Take responsibility for yourself! Make something of yourself!" But with what raw materials are the poor to make something of themselves?

People love to say, "Give a man a fish, and he'll eat for a day. Teach a man to fish, and he'll eat for a lifetime." What they don't say is, "And it would be nice if you gave him a fishing rod." That's the part of the analogy that's missing. Working with Andrew was the first time in my life I realised you need someone from the privileged world to come to you and say, "Okay, here's what you need, and here's how it works." Talent alone would have gotten me nowhere without Andrew giving me the CD writer. People say, "Oh, that's a handout." No. I still have to work to profit from it. But I don't stand a chance without it. One afternoon I was in my room making a CD when Bongani came over to pick up his inventory. He saw me mixing songs on my computer.

"This is insane," he said. "Are you doing this live?"

"Yeah."

"Trevor, I don't think you understand; you're sitting on a gold mine. We need to do this for a crowd. You need to come to the township and start DJing gigs. No one has ever seen a DJ playing on a computer before."

Bongani lived in Alexandra. Where Soweto is a sprawling, government-planned ghetto, Alexandra is a tiny, dense pocket of a shantytown, left over from the pre-apartheid days. Rows and rows of cinder-block and corrugated-iron shacks, practically stacked on top of one another. Its nickname is Gomorrah because it has the wildest parties and the worst crimes. Street parties are the best thing about Alexandra. You get a tent, put it up in the middle of the road, take over the street, and you've got a party. There's no formal invitations or guest list. You just tell a few people, word of mouth travels, and a crowd appears. There are no permits, nothing like that. If you own a tent, you have the right to throw a party in your street. Cars creep up to the intersection and the driver will see the party blocking their way and shrug and make a U-turn. Nobody gets upset. The only rule is that if you throw a party in front of somebody's house, they get to come and share your alcohol. The parties don't end until someone gets shot or a bottle gets broken on someone's face. That's how it has to end; otherwise, it wasn't a party. Back then, most DJs could spin for only a few hours; they were limited by the number of vinyls they could buy. Since parties went all night, you might need five or six DJs to keep the dancing going. But I had a massive hard drive stuffed with MP3s, which is why Bongani was excited when he saw me mixing—he saw a way to corner the market.

"How much music do you have?" he asked.

"Winamp says I can play for a week."

"We'll make a fortune."

Our first gig was a New Year's Eve party the summer we graduated from Sandringham. Bongani and I took my tower, my giant monitor, and all the cables and the keyboard and the mouse. We loaded everything up in a minibus and brought it over to Alex. We took over the street in front of his house, ran the electricity out of his place, set up the computer, set up speakers, and borrowed a tent, and people came. It was explosive. By midnight the whole street was packed from one end to the other. Ours was the biggest New Year's Eve party in Alexandra that year, and to have the biggest party in Alexandra is no joke. All night, from far and wide, people kept coming. The word spread: "There's a light-skinned guy who plays music on a computer. You've never seen anything like it." I DJ'd by myself until dawn. By then me and my friends were so drunk and exhausted that we passed out on the lawn outside Bongani's house.

The party was so big it made our reputation in the hood, instantly. Pretty soon we were getting booked all over. When Bongani and I graduated from high school, we were unable to find work. There were no available jobs for us. The only ways I could make money were by pirating CDs and DJing parties, and now that I'd moved away from Sandringham, the minibus drivers and corner kids in Alexandra were the single largest market for my CDs. It was also where I was getting the most gigs, so I naturally gravitated there to keep earning. The majority of the white students I knew were taking a gap year. "I'm going to take a gap year and travel around Europe." That's what the white kids said. "I, too, am going to take a gap year," I explained. I'm going to spend a year in the township, hanging out on the corner." That's exactly what I did. Every day, Bongani and I and our team would go sit on the low brick wall that ran down the middle of the road in front of Bongani's house in Alex. I'd bring my CDs with me. We'd listen to music and rehearse our dance movements. We sold CDs during the day and DJed events at night. We began to be booked for shows in different townships and hoods. I was able to obtain unique tunes that few others had access to thanks to my computer and modem, but this presented a problem for me. When I played the new music at events, people would gather and ask, "What is this?" "How do you move to it?" For example, suppose a DJ plays the song "Watch Me (Whip/Nae Nae)"—it's a catchy song, but what is a whip? What exactly is a nae nae? To make that song famous, you must know how to whip and nae nae; new music only works at parties if people know how to dance to it. Bongani felt that we required a dance team to demonstrate the moves to the tunes we were playing. Because we spent our days listening to CDs and making up dance moves, our crew from the corner already knew all the songs, so they became our dancers. And the crew's greatest, most beautiful, and most elegant dancer was Bongani's neighbour, Hitler.

Hitler was a dear friend of mine, and that man could dance. He was fascinating to watch. He moved with a looseness and fluidity that defied physics—imagine a jellyfish walking on ground. Incredibly attractive as well, tall and slender and muscular, with lovely, smooth skin, huge teeth, and a terrific smile that never stops laughing. And he did nothing but dance. He'd wake up in the morning, blasting house music or hip-hop, and spend the rest of the day perfecting movements. Everyone in the hood knows who the best dancer in the squad is. He's like a status symbol for you. You don't have a car or great clothes when you're poor, but the best dancer gets chicks, so that's the guy you want to roll with. Hitler was our saviour. There were dance competitions during the parties. Kids from all over would gather and bring their greatest dances. We'd bring Hitler every time, and he almost always won. When Bongani and I were putting together a performance for our dancing crew, there was little doubt about who would be the main attraction. We designed the entire scene around Hitler. I'd warm up the audience with a few songs before bringing out the dancers for a couple of routines. Once the celebration got going, they'd form a semicircle around the stage, with a gap in the back for Hitler to enter. I'd blast Redman's "Let's Get Dirty" and start pumping up the crowd even more. "Are you prepared?! I'm not hearing you! Make some noise, let me hear it!" People would yell, and Hitler would leap into the centre of the semicircle, causing the throng to erupt. Hitler would do his thing while the guys surrounded him and cheered him on. Hitler, although an unusual name, is not unheard-of in South Africa. Part of it has to do with the way a lot of black people pick names. Black people choose their traditional names with great care; those are the names that have deeply personal meanings. But from colonial times through the days of apartheid, black people in South Africa were required to have an English or European name as well—a name that white people could pronounce, basically. So you had your English name, your traditional name, and your last name: Patricia Nombuyiselo Noah. Nine times out of ten, your European name was chosen at random, plucked from the Bible or taken from a Hollywood celebrity or a famous politician in the news. I know guys named after Mussolini and Napoleon. And, of course, Hitler. Westerners are shocked and confused by that, but really it's a case of the West reaping what it has sown. The colonial powers carved up Africa, put the black man to work, and did not properly educate him. White people don't talk to black people. So why would black people know what's going on in the white man's world? Because of that, many black people in South Africa don't really know who Hitler was. My own grandfather thought "a hitler" was a kind of army tank that was helping the Germans win the war. Because that's what he took from what he heard on the news. For many black South Africans, the story of the war was that there was someone called Hitler and he was the reason the Allies were losing the war. This Hitler was so powerful that at some point black people had to go help white people fight against him—and if the white man had to stoop to ask the black man for help fighting someone, that someone must be the toughest guy of all time. So if you want your dog to be tough, you name your dog Hitler. If you want your kid to be tough, you name your kid Hitler. There's a good chance you've got an uncle named Hitler. It's just a thing.

At Sandringham, we were taught more about World War II than the typical black kids in the townships were, but only in a basic way. We weren't taught to think critically about Hitler and anti-Semitism and the Holocaust. We weren't taught, for instance, that the architects of apartheid were big fans of Hitler, that the racist policies they put in place were inspired, in part, by the racist policies of the Third Reich. We weren't taught how to think about how Hitler related to the world we lived in. We weren't being taught to think, period. All we were taught was that in 1939 Hitler invaded Poland and in 1941 he invaded the Soviet Union and in 1943 he did something else. They're just facts. Memorise them, write them down for the test, and forget them. There is also this to consider: The name Hitler does not offend a black South African because Hitler is not the worst thing a black South African can imagine. Every country thinks their history is the most important, and that's especially true in the West. But if black South Africans could go back in time and kill one person, Cecil Rhodes would come up before Hitler. If people in the Congo could go back in time and kill one person, Belgium's King Leopold would come way before Hitler. If Native Americans could go back in time and kill one person, it would probably be Christopher Columbus or Andrew Jackson. I often meet people in the West who insist that the Holocaust was the worst atrocity in human history, without question. Yes, it was horrific. But I often wonder, with African atrocities like in the Congo, how horrific were they? The thing Africans don't have that Jewish people do have is documentation. The Nazis kept meticulous records, took pictures, made films. And that's really what it comes down to. Holocaust victims count because Hitler counted them. Six million people were killed. We can all look at that number and rightly be horrified. But when you read through the history of atrocities against Africans, there are no numbers, only guesses. It's harder to be horrified by a guess. When Portugal and Belgium were plundering Angola and the Congo, they weren't counting the black people they slaughtered. How many black people died harvesting rubber in the Congo? In the gold and diamond mines of the Transvaal?

So in Europe and America, yes, Hitler is the Greatest Madman in History. In Africa he's just another strongman from the history books. In all my time hanging out with Hitler, I never once asked myself, "Why is his name Hitler?" His name was Hitler because his mom named him Hitler. We blew up when Bongani and I introduced dancers to our DJ sets. Our group was known as the Black and White Boys. The Springbok Boys were the dancers. We began to be booked everywhere. Successful black families were relocating to the suburbs, but their children still wanted to have block parties and be a part of the township culture, so they hired us to play at their events. Word of mouth spread. We were soon obtaining more and more bookings in the suburbs, meeting and playing for white people.

One boy from the township we knew, his mother, was interested in developing cultural activities for schools. In America, they'd be referred to as "diversity programs." They were springing up all throughout South Africa because, in this post-apartheid period, we were meant to be learning about and embracing one another. This kid's mother asked whether we wanted to participate in a cultural day at a school in Linksfield, a rich area south of Sandringham where my friend Teddy resided. There would be many types of dancing and music, and everyone would come together to socialise and be cultural. We agreed since she offered to pay. She supplied us with the details, including the time and location, as well as the name of the school: the King David School. A Jewish institution.

We reserved a minibus on the day of the event, loaded it with our belongings, and drove over. We sat in the rear of the school's assembly hall and watched the performances that went onstage before us; flamenco dancers, Greek dancers, and traditional Zulu musicians all took turns performing. Then we were on our feet. The Hip Hop Pantsula Dancers—the South African B-Boys—were our moniker. Onstage, we set up our sound system. When I looked around, the entire hall was filled with Jewish kids wearing yarmulkes and eager to celebrate.

I took up the microphone. "Are you ready to rock out?!"

"Yeahhhhhh!"

"Make some noise!" says the narrator.

"Yeahhhhhh!"

I began to play. My gang was dancing, the bass was thumping, and everyone was having a good time. The teachers, chaperones, parents, and hundreds of children were all dancing wildly. Our act was planned for fifteen minutes, and at the ten-minute mark, I played "Let's Get Dirty," brought out my star dancer, and shut down.

I started the song, the dancers formed a semicircle, and I took the mic.

"Are you guys ready?!"

"Yeahhhhhh!"

"You people aren't prepared! "Are you prepared?"

"Yeeeaaaahhh!"

"OK, fine! Give it up and make some noise for HIIIIIITTTT RRRRRRRRRRRRR!!!"

Hitler jumped into the centre of the circle and began slaughtering it. "Go Hit-ler! Go Hit-ler! Go Hit-ler! Go Hit-ler!" the guys around him chanted. They were bouncing to the beat with their arms out in front of them. "Go, Hit-ler! Go, Hit-ler! Go, Hit-ler!" And I was right there on the mic, directing them. "Go Hit-ler, Hit-ler!" Hit-ler, Hit-ler, Hit-ler!"

The entire room came to a halt. There was no one dancing. The instructors, chaperones, parents, and hundreds of Jewish children in yarmulkes all froze and peered up at us on stage. I was completely unaware. Hitler was as well. We continued on our journey. The only sound in the room for around thirty seconds was the beat of the music and me on the mic saying, "Go Hit-ler! Hit-ler, go! Hit-ler, go! Put your hands up for Hitler, yo!"

An instructor came up behind me and ripped my system's plug from the wall. The hall fell silent, and she turned to face me, enraged. "How could you?! This is revolting! You hideous, filthy, awful beast! What are you thinking?!"

My mind was racing as I tried to figure out what she was on about. Then it hit me. Hitler had a signature dance motion known as o spana va. It means "where you work" and is quite sexual: His hips would sway and thrust, as if he were fucking the air. That was the move he was doing when the teacher ran out, so clearly it was the dancing that she found repulsive. However, this is a common move among Africans. It's ingrained in our culture. This woman was calling us nasty when we were sharing our culture for a cultural day. She was outraged, and I was offended that she was offended.

"Lady," I told her, "I think you need to calm down."

"I'm not going to calm down!" "How dare you come here and offend us?"

"This is not meant to offend anyone. This is our identity!"

"Get the hell out of here!" "You people are revolting."

And there you have it. You guys. Now I understood what was going on: this person was racist. She couldn't look at black males dancing suggestively and not get irritated. We were arguing as I was packing my belongings.

"Pay attention, lady. We're now free. We're going to do what we're going to do. You won't be able to stop us."

"I'll just let you know that my people have stopped people like you before, and we can stop you again."

Of course, she was talking about stopping the Nazis during WWII, but that wasn't what I was hearing. In South Africa, Jews are merely white people. All I could hear was this white lady yelling about how white people had previously beaten us and would do so again. "You will never stop us again, lady," I responded, and then played the trump card: "You will never stop us, because now we have Nelson Mandela on our side!" And he told us we could do it!"

"What?!"

She was perplexed. I'd had enough. I began cursing her out. "Screw you, lady. Fuck your show. Screw your school. Fuck your entire people. Let's go, fellas! We're leaving!"

We did not leave that school. We danced our way out. We danced down the street, hands pumping in the air. "Go, Hit-ler! Go, Hit-ler! Go, Hit-ler!" Because Hitler had shut down shit. Hitler had the most gangster dancing moves ever, and those white people were taken aback.

CHAPTER 8

THE CHEESE BOYS

Bongani, my pal, was a short, balding, super-buff guy. He wasn't always like this. He'd been scrawny his entire life until a bodybuilding magazine landed in his hands and changed his life. Bongani was the type of person that brought out the best in everyone. He was that friend who saw your potential and believed in you when no one else did, which is why so many of the township kids gravitated toward him, and why I gravitated toward him as well. Bongani was always popular, but his reputation skyrocketed after he beat up one of the school's most notorious bullies. That established his position as the township kids' leader and protector. Bongani resided in Alex, but I never went there while we were still in school; instead, he'd come to my house in Highlands North. I'd gone to Alex a few times for quick visits, but I'd never spent any significant amount of time there. Let's just say I'd never been there at night. Going to Alex during the day is not the same as going there at night. Gomorrah was given its name for a purpose. Bongani approached me on the quad one day after school, not long before we matriculated.

"Hey, let's go to the neighbourhood," he suggested.

"The neighbourhood?"

I had no idea what he was talking about at first. I was familiar with the term "hood" from rap music, and I was familiar with the various townships where black people resided, but I had never used one to describe the other. Apartheid barriers were falling just as American hip-hop was exploding, and hip-hop made it cool to be from the hood. Previously, living in a township was something to be embarrassed of; it was the pits. Then there were films like Boyz n the ghetto and Menace II Society, which made the ghetto look hip. The characters in those films and songs owned it. Township kids began to do the same, wearing their identity as a badge of honour: you were no longer from the township—you were from the hood. Living in Highlands North gave you far less street cred than being from Alex. So when Bongani remarked, "Let's go to the hood," I wondered what he meant. I was curious to learn more. When Bongani took me to Alex, we entered from the Sandton side, as most people do. You ride through one of Johannesburg's wealthiest areas, through gorgeous residences and massive sums of money. Then you pass through Wynberg's industrial belt, which separates the rich and white from the impoverished and black. The massive minibus rank and bus station are located near the entrance of Alex. It's the same frantic, chaotic third-world bazaar seen in James Bond and Jason Bourne films. It's like Grand Central Station, but outside. Everything is in motion. Everything is moving. Nothing feels like it was there yesterday, nothing feels like it will be there tomorrow, but it looks the same every day. Of course, there's a KFC right next to the minibus station. One thing about South Africa is that there is always a KFC nearby. KFC discovered the black people. KFC did not engage in any games. They were in the neighbourhood before McDonald's, Burger King, or anyone else. KFC's response was, "Yo, we're here for you."

You're in Alex proper once you've passed the minibus rank. I've only gone to a few places where the electricity is as strong as it is in Alex. All day long, it's a hive of nonstop human activity, with people coming and going, criminals hustling, guys on the corner doing nothing, and children running around. Because there is nowhere for all that energy to go and no mechanism for it to dissipate, it erupts on a regular basis in spectacular acts of violence and insane parties. One minute it'll be a peaceful afternoon with folks hanging out and doing their thing, then the next thing you know, a patrol car is chasing gangsters through the streets, a gun war is raging, and helicopters are buzzing overhead. Then, five minutes later, it's as if nothing happened—everyone is back to hanging out, back to hustling, coming and going, rushing about. Alex is organised on a grid, with a network of avenues. Although the streets are paved, the walkways are largely made of dirt. The colour palette consists of cinder block and corrugated iron, grey and dark grey, with vibrant pops of colour. Someone has painted a lime green wall, or there is a bright-red sign above a takeaway store, or perhaps someone has picked up a bright-blue piece of sheet metal by chance. There isn't much in the way of basic sanitation. Trash is everywhere, and there is usually a garbage fire on some side street. Something is always on fire in the hood.

Every imaginable smell can be found as you walk. In the streets, people are cooking and eating takeaways. Some family has a shack that has been jury-rigged onto the back of someone else's shack, and they don't have running water, so they bathe in a bucket from the outdoor tap and then dump the dirty water in the street, where it runs into the river of sewage that is already there because the water system has backed up again. There's a mechanic who thinks he knows what he's doing but doesn't. He's dumping old motor oil into the street, which is now mingling with dirty bathwater to form a river of filth running down the street. There's almost certainly a goat around—there's always a goat. As you travel, sound floods over you, a steady thrum of human activity, people chatting, haggling, and arguing in a dozen different languages. There is always music playing. Traditional South African music is booming from one corner, Dolly Parton is screaming from the next, and someone is driving by pumping the Notorious B.I.G. For me, the hood was a sensory overload, yet amid the chaos, there was order, a system, and a social hierarchy based on where you lived. First Avenue was unpleasant due to its proximity to the ruckus of the minibus rank. Second Avenue was lovely since it contained semi-detached houses built when there was still some sort of organised settlement in place. Third, Fourth, and Fifth Avenues were more upscale—at least for the township. These were the old money, the established families. Then it got truly shady from Sixth Avenue on down, with more shacks and shanties. There were a few schools and soccer grounds nearby. There were a few hostels, massive government projects built to house migrant workers. You had no desire to go there. That's where the real thugs were. You went there only if you required an AK-47.

After Twentieth Avenue, you came to the Jukskei River, and on the other side, across the Roosevelt Street Bridge, was East Bank, the newest and prettiest area of town. The government had gone into the East Bank, wiped out the squatters and their shacks, and begun to build permanent dwellings. It was still low-income housing, but it was a nice two-bedroom home with small yards. The families that resided there had some money and normally sent their children to better schools, such as Sandringham. Bongani's parents lived in East Bank, at the junction of Roosevelt and Springbok Crescent, and we ended up there after going from the minibus rank through the hood, sitting around outside his house on the low brick wall down the centre of Springbok Crescent, doing nothing and shooting the crap. I didn't realise it at the time, but I was about to spend the next three years of my life hanging around in that very location. My stepfather had made my home life toxic by the time I graduated from high school at the age of seventeen. I didn't want to remain there any longer, and my mother agreed that I should leave. She assisted me in moving to a cheap, roach-infested flat in a nearby building. My plan, to the extent that I had one, was to attend university and become a computer programmer, but we couldn't pay the tuition. I needed to earn some money. Selling unlicensed CDs was the only way I knew how to get money, and one of the best areas to sell CDs was in the hood, because that's where the minibus rank was. Minibus drivers were continuously on the lookout for new tunes because having good music was one of the ways they drew clients. Another appealing aspect of the hood is its low cost. You can survive on almost nothing. A kota is a type of food available in the neighbourhood. It's half a loaf of bread. Scrape out the bread, then stuff it with fried potatoes, a slice of baloney, and achar, a pickled mango relish. That will set you back a couple of rands. The more cash you have, the more enhancements you can purchase. If you have a little extra cash, you can add a hot dog. If you have leftovers, you can add a genuine sausage, such as a bratwurst, or a fried egg. With all of the enhancements, the largest one can feed three people.

The ultimate upgrade for us was to add a slice of cheese. Because cheese was so pricey, it was always the thing. The hood operated on the cheese standard, not the gold standard. Cheese was money on anything. If you got a burger, that was okay, but getting a cheeseburger signified you had more money than the man who just had a hamburger. Cheese on a sandwich, cheese in the fridge, indicated that you were living the good life. If you had a little money in any South African township, folks would say, "Oh, you're a cheese boy." In other words, you're not truly a hood because your family can afford cheese. Because Bongani and his friends lived on the East Bank, they were dubbed "cheese boys" in Alex. They were looked down on as the scruff of East Bank since they lived on the first street just across the river, while the kids in the finer houses higher up on East Bank were the cheesier cheese lads. Bongani and his merry band would never profess to being cheese lads. "We're not cheese," they'd say. "We're the hood." "Eh, you're not good," the true hood people would say. "You're a piece of cheese." "We're not cheese," Bongani's men would declare as they pointed up the East Bank. "They're made of cheese." It was all a bunch of nonsense about who was hood and who was cheese.

Bongani was his crew's captain, the one who brought everyone together and got things rolling. Mzi, Bongani's henchman, was also present. Small person, just wanted to be a part of it. Bheki was the beverages man, always procuring us booze and making excuses to drink. There was also Kakoatse. G was his nickname. Mr. Pleasant. G was just interested in ladies. He was in the game if women were involved. Finally, there was Hitler, the life and soul of the party. Hitler simply desired to dance. When apartheid ended, the cheese boys found themselves in an unusually messed up predicament. It's one thing to be born in the hood and to know you'll never leave. But the cheese kid has seen the outer world. His family has fared well. They own a home. They've sent him to a good school; perhaps he's even enrolled. He has greater promise, but he has not been given more opportunities. He has been made aware of the world beyond, but he has not been given the means to access it. Technically, the unemployment rate in South Africa was "lower" during apartheid, which makes sense. Slavery existed—it was how everyone was employed. When democracy arrived, everyone was required to be paid a minimum salary. The cost of labour increased, and millions of people were suddenly out of work. Following apartheid, the unemployment rate for young black men skyrocketed, reaching as high as 50% in some cases. A lot of males finish high school and can't afford university, and even little retail jobs can be difficult to get by when you're from the hood and look and talk a certain way. So, for many young males in South Africa's townships, freedom looks like this: they wake up every morning, their parents may or may not go to work. Then they go outside and spend the entire day talking stuff on the corner. They're free, and they've learned to fish, but no one will give them a fishing pole.

One of the first things I learnt in the hood was that the line between civilian and criminal is extremely thin. We prefer to think we live in a world where there are good guys and bad ones, and it's easier to believe that in the suburbs because getting to know a career criminal is impossible. But then you go to the hood and notice how many hues there are in between.

Gangsters were your buddies and neighbours in the hood. You were familiar with them. You ran into them on the street and saw them at gatherings. They existed in your reality. You knew them before they became thugs. It wasn't something like, "Hey, that's a crack dealer." It was something like, "Oh, little Jimmy's selling crack now." The strange thing about these gangsters was that they all appeared to be identical. They were both driving the same red sports car. They both dated the same stunning eighteen-year-old girls. It was peculiar. It was as if they didn't have personalities; instead, they shared one. One might be the other, and the other might be the first. They'd all trained to be that thug. Even if you're not a hardcore criminal, crime is a part of your existence in the hood. There are many degrees of it. It includes everyone from a mom buying food that fell off the back of a truck to feed her family to gangs selling military-grade weaponry and hardware. The hood taught me that crime works because it does what the government does not: it cares. Crime starts at the ground level. Crime targets young children who require assistance and a helping hand. Crime provides internship programs, summer jobs, and advancement possibilities. Crime infiltrates the community. Crime makes no distinctions. My criminal career began modestly, peddling copied CDs on the street corner. That was a crime in and of itself, and I feel like I owe all these artists money for taking their music, but by hood standards, it wasn't even criminal. It never occurred to any of us at the time that we were doing anything wrong—if copying CDs is illegal, why do they produce CD players?

Bongani's house's garage opened onto Springbok Crescent. We'd open the doors every morning, run an extension cord out into the street, set up a table, and play music. People passing by would inquire, "What is that?" "Could I please have one?" Our area was also where many minibus drivers concluded their routes and looped back to the minibus rank. They'd stop by, place an order, and then return to pick it up. Swing by, place an order, and return to pick it up. We spent the entire day racing out to them, returning to the garage to prepare more mixtures, and returning to sell. When we got tired of the wall, we'd go hang out in a converted shipping container around the corner. It had a pay phone inside that we would use to call folks. We'd stroll back and forth between the container and the wall when things were slow, talking and hanging out with the other individuals who had nothing to do in the middle of the day. We'd speak with drug traffickers and thugs. The cops would come bursting through every now and again. A typical day in the life of a hoodlum. The next day, the same thing happened. Because Bongani understood all the possibilities and knew how to use them, selling gradually evolved into hustling. Bongani, like Tom, was a hustler. Whereas Tom was only interested in the short con, Bongani had plans: if we do this, we get that, and then we can trade that for the other item, giving us the leverage we need to get something bigger. Some minibus drivers, for example, were unable to pay in whole. "I don't have the money because I just started working," they'd explain. "However, I require new music." Can I give you folks some credit? I'll have to give you a ride. I'll pay you at the end of the week, at the completion of my shift?" So we began allowing drivers to buy on credit while charging them a little interest fee. We began to earn more money. Never more than a few hundred, perhaps a thousand rand at a time, but it was all cash. Bongani was quick to recognize our predicament. Everyone in the neighbourhood requires money. Everyone is seeking a short-term loan to pay a payment, pay a fine, or simply hold things together. People began approaching us and requesting money. Bongani would strike a bargain and then come to me. "Hey, we're going to make a deal with him." We'll lend him a hundred dollars, and he'll repay us one-twenty dollars at the end of the week." Okay, I'd say. The man would then return and offer us 120 rand. Then we repeated the process. Then we did it again. We began by doubling our money, then tripling it. Cash also provided us with leverage in the hood's barter economy. It's common knowledge that if you're standing on a main street corner in the hood, someone will try to sell you something. "Man, man, man. Yo, yo, yo." "Would you like some weed?" "Would you like to buy a VCR?" "Do you want to buy a DVD player?" "Yo, I'm selling a TV." That's exactly how it works.

Let's imagine we see two individuals bargaining on the corner, one a crackhead attempting to sell a DVD player and the other a working dude who wants it but doesn't have the money because he hasn't received his pay yet. They're back and forth, but the crackhead needs the money right now. Crackheads are impatient. With a crackhead, there is no such thing as a layaway plan. So Bongani intervenes and takes the working man aside.

"Look, I know you can't afford the DVD player right now," Bongani says. "But how much money are you willing to pay for it?"

"I'll pay one-twenty," he offers.

"Okay, cool."

The crackhead is then taken aside by Bongani.

"How much money do you want for the DVD player?"

"I want a one-forty."

"All right, listen up. You're a drug addict. This is a thief's DVD player. I'm going to give you fifty dollars."

The crackhead complains briefly before accepting the money since he's a crackhead, it's cash, and crack is all about the present. Then Bongani returns to the working man.

"OK, OK. We'll go with one-twenty. This is your DVD player. It's all yours."

"But I don't have the one-twenty."

"It's fine. You can take it now, but instead of one-twenty, give us forty when you get paid."

"Okay."

So we've spent 50 rand on the crackhead and received 140 from the working guy. Bongani, on the other hand, would see a way to flip it and grow it again. Assume the person who purchased the DVD player worked in a shoe store.

"How much do you pay for a pair of Nikes with your staff discount?" Bongani would inquire.

"I can get a pair of Nikes for one-fifty."

"Okay, instead of giving us one-forty, we'll give you ten, and you get us a pair of Nikes with your discount."

So this guy walks away with a DVD player and a tenner in his pocket. He believes he got a terrific deal. He gets us the Nikes, and then we go to one of East Bank's cheesier cheese lads and say, "Yo, dude, we know you want the new Jordans." There are 300 of them in the stores. We'll sell them to you for $200." We sold him the sneakers and have now converted 60 rand into 200 rand. That's the neighbourhood. Someone is always buying and someone is always selling, and the hustle is all about trying to be in the middle of it all. Nothing was lawful. Nobody had any idea where anything originated from. Did the person who gave us the Nikes truly have a "staff discount"? You have no idea. You don't inquire. "Hey, look what I found" and "Cool, how much do you want?" That is the international standard. I didn't know what to ask at first. I recall buying a car stereo or something similar once.

"But who did this belong to?" I wondered.

"Eh, don't worry about it," said one of the guys. "White people have health insurance."

"Insurance?"

"Yeah, when white people lose stuff, they have insurance policies that pay them cash for what they've lost, so it's like they've lost nothing."

"Oh, okay," I replied. "That sounds nice."

And that was the extent of our consideration: when white people lose things, they get money, just another pleasant perk of being white. It's easy to pass judgement on crime when you're fortunate enough to be immune to it. But the ghetto taught me that everyone has different ideas about what is right and wrong, what defines crime, and how much criminality they are ready to participate in. If a crackhead comes through with a crate of Corn Flakes boxes he stole from the rear of a supermarket, the poor mom isn't thinking, "I'm helping a criminal by buying these Corn Flakes." No. She thinks, My family needs food, and this guy has Corn Flakes, so she buys them. My own mother, my super-religious, law-abiding mother who used to lecture me about breaking the laws and learning to behave, I'll never forget coming home to a large package of frozen burger patties from a takeaway shop called Black Steer. At Black Steer, a burger costs at least 20 rand.

"What in the hell is this?" I said.

"Oh, I think some guy at work had these and was selling them," she explained. "I got a great deal."

"But where did he get it from?"

"I'm not sure. He claimed to know someone who—"

"Mom, he stole it."

"We don't know anything about that."

"We are aware of this. Where in the world is this person going to get all of these burger patties at random?"

We, of course, ate the burgers. Then we gave thanks to God for the supper. When Bongani originally remarked, "Let's go to the hood," I assumed we were going to sell CDs and throw DJ parties. We discovered that we were selling CDs and DJing parties to fund a payday loan and pawnshop business in the neighbourhood. That rapidly became our primary focus. Every day was the same in the hood. I'd get up early. Bongani would meet me at my apartment and we'd take a minibus to Alex with my computer, hauling the massive tower and the massive, hefty monitor the entire journey. We'd set it up in Bongani's garage and start making CDs. Then we'd go for a walk. We'd have breakfast at the corner of Nineteenth and Roosevelt. Food is an area where you must exercise caution when trying to stretch your budget. You must plan or your gains will be eaten. So for breakfast every morning, we eat vetkoek, which is just fried dough. Those were cheap, at 50 cents each. We could buy a bunch of those and have enough energy to get us through the rest of the day.

Then we'd dine on the street corner. We'd take orders from the minibus drivers as they passed by as we ate. Then we'd go back to Bongani's garage and listen to music, lift weights, and make CDs. The drivers would begin returning from their morning trips about ten or eleven a.m. We'd take the CDs and head out to the corner where they could pick up their belongings. Then we'd simply sit out on the corner, meeting people, seeing who came by, and seeing where the day would lead us. This is something a man requires. That's being sold by a man. You never knew what it would be. At lunch, there was always a surge of business. We'd be all throughout Alexandra, stopping at different businesses and corners and haggling with everyone. We'd obtain free rides from minibus drivers because we'd hop in with them and utilise the opportunity to discuss what music they needed, but we were covertly riding with the guy for free. "Hey, we'd want to take orders. While you're driving, we'll talk to you. What do you require? What kind of music are you looking for? Is the new Maxwell required? Okay, we now have the new Maxwell. Okay, we'll speak with you later. We'll break out here." Then we'd get on another ride to wherever we needed to go next.

After lunch, business would slow down, and we'd get our lunch, which was usually the lowest item we could purchase, such as a smiley with some corn meal. A smiley is the head of a goat. They've been cooked and seasoned with chilli pepper. We call them smileys because when you've eaten all of the flesh, the goat appears to be smiling at you from the platter. The cheeks and tongue are delightful, but the eyes are revolting. They dissolve in your mouth. You put the eyeball in your teeth and bite it, and it pops like a ball of pus. It lacks crunch. It has no bite. It has no appealing flavour in any way. We'd go back to the garage after lunch to unwind, sleep off the food, and make more CDs. We'd see a lot of moms in the afternoons. Our mothers adored us. They were among our most loyal consumers. Moms are the ones wanting to buy that box of soap that dropped off the back of the truck, and they're more likely to buy it from us than from some crackhead. Dealing with crackheads is a horrible experience. We were respectable, well-spoken East Bank boys. Because we provided that layer of respectability to the transaction, we could even charge a premium. Moms are frequently the most in need of short-term loans to pay for various family expenses. They'd rather deal with us than some gangster loan shark, yet again. Moms knew we wouldn't break anyone's legs if they didn't pay. That was not anything we believed in. Let's not forget that we weren't capable of it. But this is when Bongani's ingenuity came into play. He always knew what a person could supply if they didn't pay.

We made some of the most bizarre exchanges. Moms in the hood are very protective of their daughters, especially if they are attractive. There were girls that were locked up in Alex. They went to school, came home, and immediately entered the house. They were not permitted to depart. Boys weren't permitted to chat to them, or even hang out in the house—none of that. "She's so beautiful," some guy would say about some locked-up chick. I'll go to any length to get with her." He couldn't, however. No one could.

That mum would then require a loan. We lent her the money, and she couldn't kick us out of her house until she paid us back. We'd stop by, visit, and make small talk. The mother couldn't yell, "Don't talk to those boys!" because her daughter would be right there. We were able to create a relationship with the mother thanks to the financing. We'd be invited to join them for supper. Once the mom saw we were good guys, she agreed to allow us to take her daughter to a party as long as we promised to return her safely. So we'd go visit the person who'd been dying to meet the daughter.

"Hey, let's work something out. We'll bring the female to your party, and you'll get to know her. "How much are you willing to give us?"

"I don't have any money," he'd explain, "but I do have some cases of beer."

"All right, so tonight is the party. "You provide us with two cases of beer for the party."

"Cool."

We'd then proceed to the party. We'd invite the daughter, who was generally overjoyed to be able to escape her mother's confinement. We'd bring the beer, he'd get to hang out with the girl, we'd pay off the mom's debt to show our appreciation, and we'd make our money back selling the beer. things were always possible to make things work. Working the angles, solving the riddle, seeing what goes where, who needs what, who we can connect with and who can then get us the money was often the most enjoyable part.

We probably had roughly 10,000 rand in capital at the peak of our work. We had loans being made and interest being paid. We had a stockpile of Jordans and DVD players that we had purchased to resale. We also had to purchase blank CDs, rent minibuses to transport us to DJ jobs, and feed five guys three times a day. On the computer, we kept track of everything. I understood how to do spreadsheets because I grew up in my mother's world. We had a

Microsoft Excel spreadsheet with everyone's names, how much they owed, when they paid, and when they didn't. When I got home from work, business started to pick up. Men coming home from work, minibus drivers picking up one last order. The men were not searching for soap and Corn Flakes. They desired the equipment—DVD players, CD players, and PlayStation games. Because they'd been hustling and thieving all day, more guys would come through peddling items. There'd be a guy selling a cellphone, another selling leather jackets, and another selling shoes. There was this one guy who resembled a black Mr. Burns from The Simpsons. He'd always come by at the end of his shift with the most bizarre useless items, such as an electric toothbrush that didn't have a charger. He once gave us an electric razor.

"What in the hell is this?"

"It's an electric razor?"

"Do you have an electric razor?" We're all black. What effect do these items have on our skin? "Do you know anyone here who knows how to use an electric razor?"

We had no idea where he got this information. Because you do not inquire. We did, however, eventually piece everything together: He was employed at the airport. He was boosting garbage from other people's suitcases. The adrenaline would gradually fade away, and we'd wind down. We'd make our last collections, check our CD stock, and balance our accounts. If there was a party to DJ that night, we'd start preparing. Otherwise, we'd get a couple beers and sit about drinking, talking about our days, and listening to gunfire in the background. Every night, gunshots rang out, and we'd try to figure out what kind of weapon it was. "That's nine-millimetre." Normally, there'd be a police chase, with patrol cars rushing through the streets after some person in a stolen automobile. Everyone would then return home for dinner with their families. I'd take my computer, board a minibus, ride home, sleep, and then return the next day to do it all over again. A year has gone by. Then there are two. I had stopped saving for college and was no closer to being able to enrol. The tough thing about the hood is that you're always working, working, working, and it feels like something is happening when nothing is. Every day from seven a.m. to seven p.m., I was out there wondering how we could transform 10 rand into twenty. How do we get from twenty to fifty? How do I multiply fifty by a hundred? We'd spend it on food and possibly some beers at the end of the day, then go home and come back with the question: "How do we turn ten into twenty?" How do we get from twenty to fifty? It took an entire day to flip the money. You have to be walking, moving, and thinking at the same time. You had to get to, find, and meet a guy. We'd finish up back at zero on many days, but I always felt like I'd been incredibly productive. Hustling is to work what Internet surfing is to reading. If you sum up how much you read on the Internet in a year—tweets, Facebook posts, lists—you've read the equivalent of a shitload of books, but in reality, you've read none. When I think about it, that's what hustling was. It's maximum effort for a small reward. This is a hamster wheel. If I had spent all of that time studying, I would have gotten an MBA. Instead, I majored in hustling, which no university would provide me a degree for.

When I first went into Alex, I was taken in by the adrenaline and thrill of it, but more importantly, I was embraced there more than anywhere else, more than in high school or anywhere else. When I first arrived, a few folks raised an eyebrow. "Who's this coloured kid?" But the hood does not pass judgement. You are welcome to attend if you so desire. I was technically an outsider in the hood because I didn't live there, but for the first time in my life, I didn't feel like one. The hood also offers a low-stress, relaxed lifestyle. All of your mental energy is focused on getting by, so you don't have to ask yourself any important questions. What exactly am I? What exactly am I supposed to be? Is what I'm doing sufficient? In the hood, being a forty-year-old man living in your mother's house and asking people for money is not frowned upon. In the hood, you never feel like a failure because someone is always worse off than you, and you never feel the desire to do more since the biggest success isn't that much higher than you, either. It enables you to exist in suspended animation. The hood also offers a tremendous sense of community. Everyone knows everyone, from the crackhead to the police officer. People look out for one another. The way things work in the hood is that if any mother asks you to do something, you must say yes. The phrase is "Can I send you?" It's as if everyone is your mother, and you are everyone's child.

"Can I send you?"

"Yeah, what do you need?"

"I need you to go buy some milk and bread."

"Yeah, that's cool."

Then she hands you money and tells you to go buy milk and bread. You don't say no as long as you aren't busy and it doesn't cost you anything. The most important thing to remember in the hood is that you must share. You cannot become wealthy on your own. Do you have any money? Why aren't you assisting others? Everyone pitches in to aid the elderly lady down the street. You go out and buy beer for everyone. You dispersed it. Everyone must understand that your success benefits the community in some way, or you will become a target. The township also polices itself. When someone is detected stealing, the township takes action. When someone is caught breaking into a house, the township takes care of them. If you're caught raping a woman, hope the police catch you before the township. People do not intervene when a woman is assaulted. There are far too many questions accompanied by a thrashing. What's the point of the argument? Who is to blame? Who initiated it? However, rape is rape. Theft is the same as stealing. You've ruined the neighbourhood. The hood seemed somehow soothing, yet comfort can be hazardous. Comfort provides both a floor and a ceiling. Our friend G was unemployed and hanging out with the rest of us in our group. He then took a job at a fashionable clothes store. Every morning, he went to work, and the boys teased him about it. We'd see him suited up and heading out, and everyone would be laughing at him. "Oh, G, look at you in your fancy clothes!" "Oh, G, you're going to see the white man today, huh?" "Oh, G, don't forget to bring back some books from the library!"

After a month of G working at the establishment, we were hanging out on the wall one morning when G came out in his slippers and socks. He wasn't dressed appropriately for work.

"What's going on, G?" "How's it going with the job?"

"Oh, I'm sorry, I don't work there anymore."

"Why?"

"They accused me of stealing something, and I got fired."

And I'll never forget thinking to myself, "He did it on purpose?" He ruined himself in order to be accepted back into the group. The hood attracts attention. It never abandons you, but it also never lets you go. Because by leaving, you are insulting the place that raised and formed you and never turned you away. And that spot will fight back. It's time to leave the hood as soon as things start going well for you. Because the hood is going to lure you back in. I'll figure it out. Someone will steal something and put it in your car, and the cops will find it—something. You are unable to remain. You believe you can. You'll start doing better and bring your hood pals out to a good bar, and then someone causes a fight, one of your friends pulls a gun, and someone gets shot, and you're left standing around wondering, "What just happened?"

The hood occurred.

One night, I was DJing a party outside of Alex, in Lombardy East, a wealthier, middle-class black area. The police were called because of the loudness. They stormed in, wearing riot gear and brandishing machine guns. That's how our cops operate. We don't have to be tiny and large. What Americans refer to as SWAT is simply our normal police. They came to find the source of the music, which was coming from me. One cop approached me while I was working on my computer and pulled out a big assault rifle on me.

"You need to turn this off right now."

"Okay, okay," I replied. "I'm shutting it down."

However, I was using Windows 95. It took an eternity to shut down Windows 95. I was closing windows and exiting programs. I had one of those large Seagate disks that was easily damaged, and I didn't want to turn off the power and maybe harm the drive. This cop obviously didn't give a damn about any of it.

"Turn it off! "Turn it off!"

"I am! I'm turning it off! I have to shut down the programs!"

The throng was becoming agitated, and the cop was becoming concerned. He aimed his rifle at the computer instead of at me. But he plainly didn't understand computers since he fired the display. The monitor exploded, but the music continued to play. There was now chaos—music was blasting and everyone was running and terrified as a result of the gunshot. I ripped the power connection from the tower to turn it off. The cops then began blasting tear gas into the throng. It has nothing to do with myself or the music. Tear gas is just what the police use to disperse gatherings in black neighbourhoods, similar to a club turning on the lights to tell everyone to go. I misplaced the hard drive. Despite the fact that the cop fired the monitor, the explosion somehow fried it. The computer continued to boot, but it was unable to read the drive. My music collection has vanished. Even if I could afford a new hard disk, it would have taken me years to amass my music library. It could not be replaced. The DJing career was over. The CD-selling business has concluded. Our team's main revenue source was suddenly cut off. All we had left was to hustle, and we hustled even harder, trying to double the money we had on hand by buying this to sell for that. We began depleting our funds and were out of gas in less than a month. Then, one evening after work, our airport friend, the black Mr. Burns, dropped by.

"Hey, look what I found," he announced.

"What've you got?"

"A video camera."

That camera will live with me forever. It was an electronic camera. We purchased it from him, and I turned it on. It was filled with photographs of a wonderful white family on vacation, and it made me feel like garbage. The other items we'd purchased had never mattered to me. Nikes, electric toothbrushes, and electric razors are just a few examples. What does it matter? Sure, someone might get fired because a pallet of Corn Flakes went missing from the grocer, but that's a long way off. You don't consider it. But this camera had a personality. I glanced through those photos, knowing how much my family photos meant to me, and I thought to myself, I haven't stolen a camera. I took someone's memories. I robbed a piece of someone's life.

It's an odd thing, but throughout two years of hustling, I never considered it a criminal. I honestly didn't think it was all that horrible. It's just things that folks discovered. White individuals are insured. Whatever rationale was available. We do horrific things to one another in society because we don't see the person we're hurting. We don't get to see their faces. We don't consider them to be people. That was the whole point of the hood in the first place: to keep apartheid victims out of sight and mind. Because if white people ever viewed black people as human beings, they would realise that slavery is unjust. We live in a world where we don't perceive the consequences of our actions because we don't live with them. It would be much more difficult for an investment banker to defraud people with subprime mortgages if he had to live with the people he was defrauding. It would never be worth it to us to commit crimes if we could see each other's anguish and empathise with one another. I never sold the camera, no matter how badly we needed the money. I felt too awful, as if it would be bad karma, which sounds silly and didn't get the family their camera back, but I couldn't do it. That camera forced me to acknowledge that there were people on the other end of what I was doing, and that what I was doing was terrible. Our crew was invited to dance in Soweto versus another crew one night. Hitler was going to compete with their best dancer, Hector, who was one of South Africa's greatest at the moment. This invitation was significant. We were going over there to represent our neighbourhood. Alex and Soweto have always been bitter rivals. Soweto was seen as the aristocratic township, whilst Alexandra was regarded as the rough and filthy slum. Hector was from Diepkloof, a good, prosperous area of Soweto. After democracy, the first million-rand residences were built in Diepkloof. "Hey, we're no longer a township." We're making great stuff right now." That was the mindset. That's who we had to contend with. Hitler practised for a week.

On the night of the dance, me and Bongani, Mzi and Bheki, G, and Hitler took a minibus to Diepkloof. Hector was the competition's winner. Then G was found kissing one of their females, which escalated into a brawl and caused everything to fall apart. Around one a.m. on our journey back to Alex, as we were heading out of Diepkloof to get on the motorway, the cops pulled our minibus over. They forced everyone to leave and searched the area. When one of the cops returned, we were waiting outside, lined up alongside the automobile.

"We've found a gun," he announced. "Whose gun is it?"

We all shook our heads.

"We don't know," we admitted.

"No, someone knows. It's someone else's rifle."

"Officer, we really don't know," Bongani said.

He smacked Bongani across the face hard.

"You're lying to me!"

Then he proceeded down the line, smacking each of us across the face and chastising us for having a pistol. We had no choice except to stand there and take it.

"You guys are trash," stated the officer. "Where are you originally from?"

"Alex."

"Oh, okay, I see." Alex has dogs. You come here and loot people, rape women, and hijack cars. "A gang of fucking hoodlums."

"No, we're dancers," she says. We're not sure—"

"I don't mind. You're all going to jail until we figure out who has the gun."

We eventually grasped what was going on. This cop was attempting to extort money from us. "Spot fine" is the euphemism that everyone uses. You perform this intricate dance with the cop in which you say the thing without saying the thing.

"Can't we do something?" you inquire.

"What exactly do you want me to do?"

"We sincerely apologise, Officer. "What are our options?"

"You tell me."

Then you're expected to make up a tale to show the cop how much money you have on you. Which we were unable to achieve due to a lack of funds. So he locked us up. It was a city bus. It could have been anyone's gun, but the only people detained were the Alex guys. Everyone else in the car might leave. The authorities took us to the police station, locked us in a cell, and then singled us out for questioning one by one. I had to give them my home location, Highlands North, when they drew me away. The officer gave me the most perplexed face.

"You're not from Alex," he pointed out. "What are you doing with these crooks?" I was at a loss for words. He locked his gaze on me. "Listen carefully, rich boy. Do you think it's entertaining to run around with these guys? This is no longer a game. I'll let you go if you tell me the truth about your pals and the gun."

When I said no, he tossed me back in jail. We stayed the night, and the next morning I called a friend, who said he could borrow money from his father to get us out. Later that day, the father arrived and paid the money. The cops continued referring to it as "bail," although it was actually a bribe. We were never arrested or processed formally. There was no documentation. Everything was alright when we got out, but it shook us. Every day, we were out in the streets, hustling, pretending to be gang members, but the truth was that we were more cheese than hood. We formed this image of ourselves as a protection mechanism to help us survive in the world we lived in. Bongani and the other East Bank boys had very little hope because of where they came from and what they looked like. In that case, you have two possibilities. You accept the retail job, flip burgers at McDonald's if you're lucky enough to get that much. The alternative is to toughen up and put up this front. Because you can't escape the ghetto, you must live by its rules. I decided to live in that world, but I wasn't born in it. I was, in fact, an imposter. On a daily basis, I was just like everyone else, but in the back of my mind, I knew I had other possibilities. I have the option of leaving. They couldn't do it.

CHAPTER 9

THE WORLD DOESN'T LOVE YOU

My mother never let me have an inch. It was tough love, lectures, discipline, and hiding whenever I got in trouble. Each and every time. For each and every offence. That is common among black parents. They're attempting to discipline you ahead of the system. "I need to do this to you before the police do it to you." Because that is all black parents worry about you from the moment you are old enough to walk out into the street, where the law awaits. Getting arrested was a way of life for Alex. It was so prevalent that we developed a sign for it out on the corner, a shorthand for clapping your wrists together like you were being put in handcuffs. Everyone understood what that meant.

"Where's Bongani?"

Clap your hands together.

"Oh, crap. When?"

"Friday at night."

"Damn."

My mother despised the hood. She didn't like my coworkers. She didn't even want them to come inside if I brought them back. "I don't like those boys," she'd complain. She didn't dislike them as individuals; she despised what they represented. "You and those boys get yourself into so much shit," she'd say. "You must be careful who you surround yourself with, because where you are can determine who you are."

The thing she despised the most about the hood was that it didn't put any pressure on me to improve. She wanted me to go to my cousin's university and hang out with him.

"What's the difference if I'm in university or the hood?" I'd say. "It's not like I'm going to a university."

"Yes, but the university's pressure will catch up with you." I recognize you. You're not going to sit back and let these folks become better than you. You will become positive and progressive if you are in a good and progressive environment. I am constantly telling you to make a change in your life, but you don't. You're going to get arrested one day, and when you do, don't contact me. I'll have the cops lock you up to teach you a lesson."

Because there were some black parents who would truly do that, not pay their child's bail or hire a lawyer for their child—the ultimate tough love. However, it does not always work because you are giving the child tough love when he may simply need affection. You're attempting to teach him a lesson, and the lesson has now become the rest of his life. I spotted an ad in the paper one morning. Some store was having a clearance sale on cell phones, and they were offering them at such a low price that I knew Bongani and I could resell them for a profit in the hood. This shop was located in the suburbs, too far away to walk and too far away to take a minibus. My stepfather's workshop and a collection of antique cars were conveniently located in our backyard. Since I was fourteen, I'd been taking Abel's junkers to travel around. I'd say I was testing them to ensure they were properly mended. That didn't strike Abel as amusing. I'd been caught many times, caught and punished by my mum. But that has never prevented me from accomplishing anything. The majority of these junkers were not street legal. They lacked valid registration and number plates. Fortunately, Abel had a stack of old licence plates in the back of the garage. I quickly discovered that I could just strap one to an old automobile and hit the road. I was nineteen, maybe twenty, and had no idea what this would lead to. I went to Abel's garage when no one was there, grabbed one of the cars, the red Mazda I'd driven to the matric dance, slapped some old plates on it, and drove off in search of cheap cell phones.

In Hillbrow, I was pulled over. When cops in South Africa pull you over, they don't give you a reason. Cops pull you over because they're cops and have the authority to do so; it's as simple as that. I used to watch movies where cops would pull people over and say things like, "You didn't signal" or "Your taillight's out." I used to wonder why American officers bother lying. One thing I like about South Africa is that we haven't honed the system to the point where we need to lie.

"Do you know why I pulled over?"

"Is it because you're a cop and I'm black?"

"You are accurate. Please, licence and registration."

When the cop pulled me over, I wanted to say something like, "Hey, I know you guys are racially profiling me!" But I couldn't make the case because I was breaking the law at the time. The cop approached my window and asked me the normal cop questions. What are your plans? Is this your vehicle? Whose vehicle is this? I was unable to respond. I went completely still. Being young, I was more concerned with getting in trouble with my parents than with the law. I'd had run-ins with cops in Alexandra and Soweto, but it was usually about the circumstances: a party being shut down, a minibus raid. The law was all around me, but it had never explicitly targeted Trevor. And when you haven't had much experience with the police, it appears rational—cops are mostly jerks, but you accept that they're doing their jobs. Your parents, on the other hand, are completely irrational.

They have been your judge, juror, and executioner your entire childhood, and it feels like they sentence you to life in prison for every misdemeanour. When I should have been afraid of the cop, all I could think was Shit shit shit; I'm going to be in big trouble when I get home.

When the cop called in the registration, he noticed that it didn't match the car. He was now firmly on my side. "This car does not belong to you! What's up with these plates?! "Get out of the car!" Only then did I realise: Ohhhhh, shit. I'm in big trouble now. When I got out of the car, he placed me in handcuffs and informed me I was being detained on suspicion of driving a stolen vehicle. He admitted to me, and the automobile was seized. The Hillbrow police station appears to be identical to every other police station in South Africa. At the height of apartheid, they were all built by the same contractor—separate nodes in a police state's central nervous system. You wouldn't know you'd moved locations if you were blindfolded and carried from one to the other. Like a hospital, they're sterile and institutional, with fluorescent lighting and poor floor tiling. My officer led me in and seated me at the front booking desk. I was charged with a crime and fingerprinted. Meanwhile, they'd been inspecting the car, which wasn't going well for me either. Whenever I took a car from Abel's workshop, I sought to take one of the junkers rather than an actual client's car; I reasoned that this would keep me out of trouble. That was a blunder. The Mazda, as one of Abel's junkers, lacked a clear claim of ownership. If it had been registered, the cops would have contacted the owner, who would have explained that the car had been dropped off for repairs, and the situation would have been resolved. I couldn't prove I hadn't stolen the car because it didn't have an owner. Carjackings were also prevalent in South Africa at the time. They were so common that no one was astonished when they occurred. You'd get a call saying a friend was coming over for dinner.

"Sorry. I was carjacked. I'm going to be late."

"Oh, that stinks. Hello, guys! Dave was robbed in his automobile."

"Sorry, Dave!"

And the party would go on. And that's if the individual survived the carjacking. They didn't always. People were constantly being shot for driving their autos. I couldn't prove I hadn't stolen the automobile, but I also couldn't prove I hadn't murdered someone for it. The cops were questioning me. "Did you murder anyone to get that car, boy?" Eh? "Are you a murderer?"

I was in big, big trouble. I only had one source of support: my parents. Everything might have been resolved with a one phone call. "Hello, this is my stepfather." He works as a mechanic. I shouldn't have borrowed his car." Done. At worst, I'd get a smack on the wrist for driving an unregistered car. But what would I get when I got home?

I sat at the police station, arrested for grand theft auto and a possible suspect in carjacking or murder, debating if I should call my parents or go to jail. With my stepfather, I was concerned that he may actually murder me. That situation seemed entirely plausible to me. When I was with my mother, I kept thinking, "She's going to make this worse." She's not the type of character witness I'm looking for right now. She is refusing to assist me. Because she had said she wouldn't. "If you ever get arrested, don't call me." I needed someone sympathetic to my situation, and I didn't think she was it. As a result, I did not contact my parents. I determined that I didn't require them. I used to be a man. I could do it on my own. I used my phone to call my cousin and tell him not to tell anyone about what had happened until I found out what to do—now all I had to do was figure out what to do.I'd been taken up late in the afternoon, so it was nearly dark by the time I was processed. Whether I liked it or not, I was spending the night in jail. At that point, a cop approached me and informed me of my situation.

The system in South Africa is that you are arrested and kept in a police station cell until your bail hearing. The judge examines your case, hears arguments from both sides, and then either dismisses the charges or sets bail and a trial date. You pay bail and go home if you can make it. However, there are numerous ways for your bail hearing to go wrong: You're assigned a lawyer who hasn't reviewed your case and has no idea what's going on. Your family is unable to pay your bail. It's possible that the court is backing down. "We're sorry, but we're too busy. There will be no further hearings today." It makes no difference why. You cannot return to jail once you have been released. If your problem is not addressed that day, you are taken to prison to await your trial. In jail, you're housed with those awaiting trial, not with the general population, but even the awaiting-trial part is dangerous because you have people picked up for traffic offences all the way up to severe offenders. You're stuck there with each other for days, weeks, or even months. It's the same in the United States. If you're poor and don't understand how the system works, you can fall between the cracks and find yourself in this strange purgatory where you're not in prison but also not not in prison. You haven't been convicted of any crime, but you're still imprisoned and unable to leave.

"Listen, you don't want to go to your bail hearing," this detective stated to me. They'll assign you a state attorney who has no idea what's going on. He won't have time for you. He'll ask the judge for a postponement, and you'll either go free or not. You don't want to do that, believe me. You have the right to stay as long as you like. You should consult with a lawyer and prepare yourself before going near a court or a judge." He wasn't offering me this counsel out of kindness for me. He struck an agreement with a defence attorney to supply him clients in exchange for a kickback. He gave me the attorney's business card, and when I called him, he agreed to take my case. He instructed me to remain seated while he handled everything. Now I needed money, because lawyers, no matter how good they are, don't work for free. I called a friend and asked him if he could approach his father for a loan. He said he'd take care of it. He spoke with his father, and the lawyer received his retainer the next day. I felt like I had things under control now that the lawyer was taken care of. I was feeling particularly slick. I'd handled the issue well, and most importantly, Mom and Abel were unaffected.

When it was time for lights out, a cop arrived and grabbed my belongings. My wallet, my belt, and my shoelaces.

"Why do you need my shoelaces?"

"So that you don't hang yourself."

"Right."

Even after he stated that, the gravity of my situation had yet to sink in. Walking to the station's holding cell and gazing around at the other six guys in there, I thought to myself, "This isn't such a big deal." Everything will be OK. I'm going to get out of here. That was my idea until the cell door clanged shut behind me and the officer roared, "Lights out!" That's when I realised, Oh, shit. This is true. The guards had handed me a scratchy blanket and a mat. I spread them out on the concrete floor and tried to relax. My mind was running over every horrible jail movie I'd ever watched. I was afraid I was going to be raped. I'm going to be raped. I'm going to be raped. But, of course, I was not raped because this was not a prison. It was jail, and there was a significant difference, as I would soon discover. I awoke the next morning with the momentary impression that everything had been a dream. Then I looked around and realised it wasn't. Breakfast arrived, and I sat down to wait. A day in jail is generally silent, interrupted only by passing guards yelling profanities at you while completing roll call. Nobody says anything inside the detention cell. Nobody enters a jail cell and says, "Hello, guys! "My name is Brian!" Because everyone is terrified, and no one wants to appear weak. Nobody wants to be the bad girl. Nobody wants to be the one who gets killed. I didn't want anyone to know I was just a kid for a traffic violation, so I went through my mind and found all the clichés of how people in prison act, and then I tried to act like that.

Everyone in South Africa knows that coloured gangsters are the most violent and savage. It's a stereotype that you've been fed your entire life. The Numbers Gangs: the 26s, 27s, and 28s are the most notorious coloured gangs. They have complete power over the prisoners. They're notorious for being brutally violent—maiming, torturing, raping, and chopping off people's heads—not to make money, but to demonstrate how cruel and terrible they are, similar to Mexican drug cartels. In fact, many of these gangs are inspired by Mexican gangs. They both wear Converse All Stars with Dickies slacks and an open shirt buttoned only at the top. By the time I was a teenager, whenever I was profiled by cops or security guards, it was usually because I appeared coloured rather than because I was black. I once went to a club with my cousin and a friend of his. Mlungisi was searched and waved in by the bouncer. He checked our guy and waved him in. Then he looked at me and got up in my face.

"Where's your knife?"

"I'm afraid I don't have a knife."

"I know you've got a knife somewhere." "Can you tell me where it is?"

He sought and searched till he gave up and allowed me in, inspecting me as if I were trouble.

"No nonsense from you!" Okay?"

I felt if I was in jail, people would assume I was the type of black person that ends up in jail, a violent criminal. So I acted it up. I took on this persona; I played the stereotype. When the cops began questioning me, I began speaking in terrible Afrikaans with a thick coloured accent. Consider a white man in America, just dark enough to pass for a Latino, strolling through a jail doing awful Mexican-gangster speech from the movies. "This is about to get crazy, ese." it's exactly what I was doing—the South African equivalent of it. This was my ingenious strategy for avoiding jail. But it was effective. They were in the cell with me for drunk driving, domestic abuse, and petty stealing. They had no notion what true African-American gangsters were like. Everyone had abandoned me.

We were all playing a game that no one was aware of. When I went in that first night, everyone gave me this look that said, "I'm dangerous." "Don't mess with me." So I said to myself, "Shit, these people are hardened criminals." I have no business being here because I am not a criminal." The next day, everything changed swiftly. As the guys went to go to their hearings, I stayed to wait for my lawyer, and more people began to arrive. I was now the veteran, performing my coloured-gangster routine and giving the new guys the identical look: "I'm dangerous." "Don't mess with me." "Shit, he's a hardened criminal," they said as they glanced at me. I shouldn't be here; I'm not like him." We went round and round. It seemed to me at one point that everyone in that cell might be faking it. We were all good people from lovely neighbourhoods with good families who had been arrested for unpaid parking tickets and other offences. We could have had a terrific time eating meals, playing cards, and discussing ladies and soccer. But that didn't happen because everyone had taken this risky stance and no one spoke because everyone was terrified of who the other guys were pretending to be. Those guys were going to walk out and go home to their families, saying, "Oh, honey, that was rough." There were some serious crooks. There was this one black man. He was a murderer, man."

I was OK after I got the game figured out. I let go. I was thinking, I've got this. This isn't a big deal. The dinner was actually rather good. They handed you these peanut butter sandwiches on large slices of bread for breakfast. Lunch consisted of chicken and rice.

The tea was excessively hot and tasted more like water than tea, but it was still palatable. There were older, hard-core inmates on their way out, and their assignment was to clean the cells and distribute books and periodicals for you to read. It was quite relaxing.

There was a time when I was eating a meal and thinking to myself, "This isn't so bad." I hang out with a lot of guys. There are no responsibilities. There are no bills to pay. There was no one bugging me or telling me what to do all the time. Sandwiches with peanut butter? Oh no, I'm addicted to peanut butter sandwiches. This is quite cool. This is something I could do. I was so terrified of the ass-whooping that awaited me at home that I seriously pondered going to prison. I thought I had a strategy for a second. "I'll go away for a couple of years, come back, and say I was kidnapped, and mom will never know, and she'll just be happy to see me."

The officers brought in the biggest man I'd ever seen on the third day. This guy was massive. Massive muscles. Skin colour is dark. Face hardened. He appeared to be capable of killing all of us. My tough-guy routines with the other prisoners—the second he walked in, our tough-guy routines were done. Everyone was scared. We were all staring at him. "Oh, fuck..."

For whatever reason, this man was half naked when the cops arrived. He was dressed in clothes that the cops had scrounge together for him at the station, a torn-up wife beater that was way too small, and slacks that were so short on him that they looked like capris. He resembled a darker version of the Incredible Hulk. This individual went to sit alone in the corner. Nobody said anything. Everyone was cautiously watching and waiting to see what he would do. Then one of the cops returned and summoned the Hulk; they required information from him. The cop began questioning him, but the man kept shaking his head and stating he didn't understand. The officer was speaking in Zulu. Tsonga was being spoken by the Hulk. The Tower of Babel was made up of black people who couldn't comprehend each other. Few people speak Tsonga in South Africa, but because my stepfather was Tsonga, I picked it up along the road. I overheard the cop and the other guy arguing and nothing getting through, so I went in and translated for them, settling things.

"If you talk to a man in a language he understands, that goes to his head," Nelson Mandela reportedly observed. When you speak to him in his language, it touches his heart." He was completely correct. When you make an attempt to learn someone else's language, even if it's just a few basic phrases, you're expressing to them, "I understand that you have a culture and identity that exists beyond me." "I see you as a person."

That is precisely what happened to the Hulk. The moment I spoke to him, this intimidating and ugly face brightened up with gratitude. "Ah, na khensa, na khensa, na khensa, na khensa." Hello, Wena Mani? Mufana wa mukhaladi u xitiela kwini xitiela kwini xiTsonga? "Who are you, kwini?" "Oh, thank you. Thank you, thank you, thank you." What is your name? How does a black man know Tsonga? "Where do you come from?"

I recognized he wasn't the Hulk when we started conversing. He was the kindest man, a gentle giant, the world's biggest teddy bear. He was unsophisticated and uneducated. I assumed he was going to commit murder, squashing a family to death with his bare hands, but it wasn't like that. He'd been arrested for stealing PlayStation games from a store. He was out of work and needed money to take home to his family, so when he heard how much these games sold for, he figured he could steal a few and sell them to white kids for a lot of money. I knew he wasn't some hardened criminal the moment he told me that. I'm familiar with the world of pirated goods—stolen videogames are worthless because it's cheaper and less hazardous to duplicate them, like Bolo's parents did.

I attempted to assist him in some way. I told him about my tactic of delaying your bail hearing to prepare your defence, so he stayed in the cell as well, biding his time, and we hit it off and hung around for a few days, having fun and getting to know each other. Nobody else in the cell understood what to make of us, the vicious coloured mobster and his scary, Hulk-like companion. He told me his story, which was all too familiar to me as a South African: The man grows up in apartheid South Africa, working on a farm as part of what amounts to a slave labour force. It's a living hell, but it's something. He gets paid a little, but he gets paid. Every waking minute of his day, he is told where to go and what to do. Then apartheid ends, and he no longer has it. He makes his journey to Johannesburg in search of a job, hoping to feed his children back home. But he's gone. He has no formal schooling. He possesses no abilities. He has no idea what to do or where he should go. The world has been indoctrinated to fear him, but the truth is that he is afraid of the world because he lacks the means to deal with it. So, what does he do now? He's a jerk. He turns into a petty thief. He has been in and out of jail. He gets lucky and finds a construction job, but then he gets laid off, and a few days later he's in a shop and sees some PlayStation games and snatches them, but he doesn't even know enough to realise he's stolen something worthless. I felt awful for him. The longer I was in jail, the more I realised that the law isn't logical at all. It's a game of chance. What is the colour of your skin? What is your financial situation? Who is your attorney? Who gets to be the judge? Theft of PlayStation games was a lesser offence than driving with invalid licence plates. He'd done something wrong, but he wasn't a criminal any more than I was. The difference was that he didn't have any friends or relatives to turn to for assistance. He had no choice except to hire a state counsel. He'd go stand in the dock, unable to speak or understand English, and everyone in the courtroom would assume the worst. He was going to go for a while and then be released with the same nothing he had when he went in. If I had to guess, he was somewhere between 35 and 40 years old, staring down another 35 to 40 years of the same.

My hearing date arrived. I bid my new acquaintance farewell and wished him the best. Then I was handcuffed and transported to the courthouse in the back of a police van to face my fate. To limit your exposure and options for escape, the holding cell where you await your hearing in South African courts is a large pen beneath the courtroom; you go up a flight of stairs into the dock rather than being escorted through the halls. In the holding cell, you're mixed in with people who have been in prison for weeks or months awaiting trial. It's an odd combination of white-collar thieves, individuals picked up on traffic stops, and true, serious criminals covered in prison tattoos. It's like the cantina scene from Star Wars, where the band is playing music and Han Solo is in the corner, and all of the bad guys and bounty hunters from all over the universe are congregating—a miserable hive of scum and villainy—except there's no music and no Han Solo. I was only with these folks for a short period of time, but I witnessed the difference between prison and jail. I saw the distinction between criminals and those who have done crimes. I could see the determination on people's faces. I remembered how naive I'd been just hours before, thinking that incarceration wasn't so horrible and that I could take it. I was suddenly terrified of what could happen to me. I was a smooth-skinned, fresh-faced young man when I entered that holding pen. I had a huge Afro at the time, and the only way to control it was to tie it back in this pretty ponytail thing. I resembled Maxwell. The soldiers shut the door behind me, and this weird old man yelled from the back, "Ha, ha, ha! Madoda, madoda! Angikaze ngibone indoda enhle kangaka enhle kangaka enhle kangaka enhle "Obuhle, Sizoba nobusuku!" "Yo! Yo! Yo!" Guys, you're a jerk. I've never seen such a stunning man. Tonight is going to be a great night!"

Fuuuuuuuuuck.

As I came in, there was a young man having a complete meltdown, talking to himself and weeping his eyes out. He looked up and locked eyes with me, as if he thought I was a kindred soul with whom he might converse. He charged at me, sobbing, about how he'd been arrested and thrown in jail, and how gangs had taken his clothes and shoes, raped him, and beaten him every day. He wasn't some thug. He was well-spoken and well-educated. He'd been waiting a year for his case to be heard; he intended to commit suicide. That person instilled terror in me.

I took a glance around the holding cell. There were easily a hundred guys in there, all spread out and huddled into their clearly and unmistakably defined racial groups: a swarm of black people in one corner, a swarm of coloured people in another, a swarm of Indians off to one side, and a swarm of white guys off to one side. The guys who'd been with me in the police van instantly, automatically went off to join the groups they belonged to the moment we got in. I became immobile. I had no idea where to go. I moved my gaze to the coloured corner. I was staring at South Africa's most known and vicious prison gang. I resembled them, yet I wasn't them. I couldn't walk over there acting like a gangster and have them find out I was a phoney. No way, no how. My friend, the game was done. The last thing I needed were black gangsters pitted against me. But what if I went to the dark alley? I know I'm black and that I identify as black, but I'm not a black person on the surface, so would the black males understand why I was walking over to them? And what kind of nonsense would I begin by getting there? Going to the black corner as a perceived coloured person may irritate the coloured gangs even more than going to the coloured corner as a phoney coloured person. Because that has been my experience my entire life. When coloured folks saw me hanging out with blacks, they would confront me and want to attack me. In the holding cell, I imagined myself initiating a race war.

"Hey! "Why are you hanging out with black people?"

"Because I am black."

"No, you aren't. "You're a colour."

"Ah, absolutely. I realise it appears that way, but bear with me as I explain. Actually, it's a funny story. Because my father is white and my mother is black, and because race is a social construct,..."

That wasn't going to happen. Not in this case. All of this was happening in my thoughts in a split second. I was making insane calculations, scanning the room, and assessing the variables. If I go here, then this will happen. If I go there, then that will happen. My entire existence flashed before me—the school playground, the Soweto spaza shops, the streets of Eden Park—every time and every place I had to be a chameleon, travel between groups, and explain who I was. It was like a high school cafeteria, only it was the high school cafeteria from hell because if I chose the incorrect table, I could be beaten, stabbed, or raped. I'd never been so terrified in my life. But I still had to make a decision. Because racism exists, and you must choose a side. You can claim that you don't take sides, but life will eventually force you to do so. That day, I chose white. They just didn't appear to be able to harm me. It was a group of ordinary, middle-aged white men. I approached them. We hung out for a while and talked a little. They were largely involved in white-collar crimes, money laundering, fraud, and racketeering. They'd be worthless if someone came over looking to cause trouble; they'd also have their asses kicked. But they had no intention of harming me. I was secure.

Fortunately, the time passed fast. I was only there for an hour before being summoned to court, where a judge would either release me or send me to prison to await trial. As I was walking away, one of the white males approached me. "Make sure you don't come back down here," he said. "Cry in front of the judge; do whatever it takes." Your life will never be the same if you get up and are sent back down."

My lawyer was waiting for me in the courtroom. Mlungisi, my cousin, was also in the gallery, ready to post my bail if things went my way.

The bailiff read out my case number, and the judge raised his head to look at me.

"How are you?" he inquired.

I had a nervous breakdown. I'd been putting on this tough-guy act for about a week and couldn't take it any longer.

"I-I'm not feeling well, Your Honor. "I'm not feeling well."

He appeared perplexed. "What?!"

"I'm not fine, sir," I explained. "I'm in a lot of pain."

"Why are you telling me this?"

"Because you asked how I was."

"Who was it that asked you?"

"You did it. "You just asked."

"I never asked, 'How are you?'" 'Who are you?' I asked. Why would I bother asking, 'How are you?'? This is a prison. I know everyone down there is in pain. If I asked everyone, 'How are you?' we would be here all day. 'Who are you?' I asked. For the record, please state your name."

"Trevor Noah."

"Okay. We can now proceed."

When the entire courtroom began to laugh, I began to laugh as well. But I was terrified now because I didn't want the judge to think I wasn't taking him seriously because I was laughing.

It turned out that I didn't need to be concerned. Everything that followed happened in a matter of minutes. My lawyer had spoken with the prosecution, and everything had been planned ahead of time. He laid out my case. I had no previous experience. I wasn't a threat. The opposing party raised no objections. My trial date was established by the judge, and I was free to go.

"Sweet Jesus, I'm never going back there again," I murmured as I walked out of court, the light of day hitting my face. It had only been a week, in a rather comfortable cell with decent meals, but a week in jail is a long, long time. A week without shoelaces is an eternity. A week without clocks or sunlight might feel like an eternity. I couldn't bear the prospect of anything worse, of serving real time in a real prison. I drove to Mlungisi's house with him, took a shower, and slept there. He dropped me off at my mother's house the next day. I took a leisurely stroll up the driveway. My objective was to claim that I had been staying with Mlungisi for a few days. I entered the house as if nothing had happened. "Hello, Mom! "How are you?" Mom said nothing and didn't ask me any questions. Okay, I thought. Cool. We're OK.

I stayed for the majority of the day. We were discussing it at the kitchen table later in the afternoon. I was narrating all these things, going on about everything Mlungisi and I had done that week, when I noticed my mother give me this look and gently shake her head. It was unlike anything I'd ever seen her deliver before. It wasn't something like, "One day, I'm going to catch you." It wasn't rage or disgust. It was a let down. She was in pain.

"What?" I said. "What exactly is it?"

"Boy, who do you think paid your bail?" she asked. Hmm? Who do you believe paid your attorney? Do you think I'm stupid? Did you expect no one to inform me?"

The truth was revealed. Of course she'd guessed: the automobile. It had gone missing the entire time. I'd been so preoccupied with avoiding incarceration and concealing my tracks that I'd forgotten the evidence of my crime was right there in the yard, the red Mazda vanished from the driveway. And, of course, when I contacted my friend, he'd asked his father for the money for the lawyer, and the father, being a parent too, had instantly called my mother. She'd given the money to my pal to pay the lawyer. She'd provided the money to my cousin to pay my bail. I'd spent the entire week in jail believing I was so cunning. But she'd been aware of everything the entire time.

"I know you see me as some crazy old bitch nagging at you," she explained, "but you forget that I ride you so hard and give you so much shit because I love you." Everything I've ever done has been motivated by love. If I don't punish you, the rest of the world will. The rest of the world does not adore you. The police do not adore you if they apprehend you. I'm attempting to save you by beating you. They're attempting to kill you when they beat you."

CHAPTER 10

MY MOTHER'S LIFE

I started gaining attention from girls for the first time after I had my hair cornrowed for the matric dance. I did, in fact, go on dates. I used to think it was because I looked better. At times, I felt it was because they enjoyed the idea that I went to the same lengths as they did to appear good. In any case, once I achieved success, I wasn't about to change the formula. Every week, I returned to the salon, spending hours getting my hair straightened and cornrowed. My mother would simply roll her eyes. "I could never date a man who spends more time on his hair than I do," she'd tell herself. Monday through Saturday, my mother worked in her office and disguised as a homeless person in her garden. Then she'd do her hair, put on a great dress, and high shoes for church, and she'd look like a million bucks. She couldn't stop tormenting me after she was dressed up, throwing tiny verbal jabs at me as we always did.

"Who's the most attractive member of the family, eh?" I hope you had a good week as the gorgeous one, because the queen is back, darling. You spent four hours at the salon to get that look. "I just got out of the shower."

She was only playing with me; no son likes to brag about how attractive his mother is. Because, to be honest, she was stunning. Beautiful on the outside, and even more so on the interior. She exuded a sense of self-assurance that I lacked. You could tell how gorgeous she was even when she was working in the garden, clad in overalls and coated in dirt.

I'm sure my mother broke a few hearts in her day, but she only had two men in her life from the time I was born: my father and my stepfather. Mighty Mechanics was a garage right around the corner from my father's house in Yeoville. Our Volkswagen was constantly breaking down, so my mother would take it there to be repaired. Abel, one of the auto technicians, was a pretty lovely man we met there. I'd run into him when we went to get the car. We went there a lot because the automobile broke down frequently. Even though there was nothing wrong with the vehicle, it eventually felt like we were there. I was maybe six or seven years old. Everything that was going on was beyond my comprehension. I just knew this guy was suddenly around. He was tall, lanky, and skinny, but he was powerful. He had lengthy arms and large hands. He had the ability to lift car engines and gears. He was attractive, yet not attractive. That was something my mother appreciated about him; she used to say there's a form of unattractiveness that ladies find appealing. She addressed him as Abie. He called her Mbuyi, an abbreviation for Nombuyiselo.

I liked him as well. Abie was charming and humorous, with a simple, gracious grin. He, too, enjoyed assisting others, particularly those in need. If a car went down on the freeway, he would pull over to see what he could do. He was the one who gave chase whenever someone cried "Stop, thief!" Did the elderly lady next door require assistance in shifting boxes? He's the one. He liked to be liked by the rest of the world, which made his abuse much more difficult to bear, because if you think someone is a monster and the rest of the world thinks he's a saint, you start to believe you're the bad one. The only conclusion you can reach is that it must be my fault that this is occurring, since why are you the only one getting his wrath?

Abel was always pleasant to me. He wasn't attempting to be my father, and my father was still in my life, so I wasn't searching for someone to take his place. That's how I imagined Mom's cool pal. He began coming out to visit us in Eden Park. Sometimes, he'd invite us to his converted garage flat in Orange Grove, which we did. Then I set fire to the white people's home, and that was the end of it. We lived together in Eden Park from then on. My mother pulled me aside during a prayer group one night.

"Hey," she called out. "I have something to tell you. "Abel and I are getting married."

Without even thinking, I answered, "I don't think that's a good idea."

I wasn't upset in any way. I just got a gut feeling about the guy. I'd sensed it long before the mulberry tree. That night hadn't changed my feelings for Abel; it had simply shown me what he was capable of in flesh and blood.

"I understand how difficult it is," she admitted. "I understand that you don't want a new dad."

"No," I replied. "No, it's not that. Abel appeals to me. I really like him. However, you should not marry him." I didn't know the word "sinister" at the time, but if I had, I would have used it. "There's just something off about him." I don't believe him. "I don't think he's a nice guy."

I'd always been fine with my mom dating this guy, but I'd never envisioned his becoming a permanent member of our family. I enjoyed being with Abel in the same way that I enjoyed playing with a tiger cub the first time I visited a tiger sanctuary: I liked it, I had fun with it, but I never considered taking it home. If we had any doubts about Abel, the answer was right in front of us all along: his name. He was Abel, the wonderful brother and son, a name straight from the Bible. And he did not disappoint. He was the firstborn, devoted, and looked after his mother and siblings. He was his family's pride and joy. But his English name was Abel. Ngisaveni was his Tsonga name. It translates as "Be afraid."

Mom and Abel tied the knot. There was no ceremony or ring exchange. They went ahead and signed the papers, and that was the end of it. Andrew, my baby brother, was born about a year later. My mother was gone for a few days, and when she returned, there was suddenly this thing in the house that cried and spit and got fed, but when you're nine years older than your sibling, their arrival doesn't change much for you. I wasn't changing diapers; I was at the shop playing arcade games and running around the neighbourhood.

For me, the most significant aspect of Andrew's birth was our first trip to meet Abel's family during the Christmas holidays. They lived in Tzaneen, a town in Gazankulu, the Tsonga homeland prior to apartheid. Tzaneen has a hot and humid tropical climate. The white farms nearby produce some of the most exquisite fruit—mangoes, lychees, and the most beautiful bananas you've ever seen. All of the fruit we export to Europe comes from there. Years of overfarming and overgrazing have devastated the soil on the black area twenty minutes down the road. Abel's mother and sisters were all traditional stay-at-home moms, and Abel and his younger brother, a police officer, provided for the family. They were all really nice and generous, and they immediately adopted us as family.

Tsonga culture is quite patriarchal, I discovered. We're talking about a future in which women must bow when greeting men. Men and women have few social encounters with one another. The men slaughter the animals, while the women prepare the feast. Men aren't even permitted in the kitchen. This was great to me as a nine-year-old boy. I was not permitted to do anything. My mother was always making me perform chores—washing the dishes, cleaning the house—but when she tried to do so in Tzaneen, the women refused.

"Trevor, make your bed," my mother would tell me.

"No, no, no, no, no," Abel's mother would say. "Trevor must go outside and play."

I was made to run away and have fun while my female step-cousins had to clean the house and assist the women in the kitchen. I was in a state of ecstasy. My mother despised every second of her presence. This trip meant a lot to Abel, a firstborn son who was bringing home his own firstborn kid. Because the father is away working in the city, the eldest son almost becomes the father/husband by default in the homelands. The man of the house is the firstborn son. He looks after his siblings. As the father's surrogate, his mother holds him in high regard. Because this was Abel's big homecoming with Andrew, he anticipated my mother to play her usual part as well. She, however, declined.

During the day, the women in Tzaneen had a variety of jobs. They made breakfast, tea, lunch, as well as the washing and cleaning. The men had been working in the city all year to support the family, so this was their vacation, sort of. They were at ease, being served by the women. They might slaughter a goat or do whatever macho activities were required, but then they would go to a men-only area and hang out and drink while the ladies cooked and cleaned. But my mother had also been working in the city all year, and Patricia Noah never stayed in anyone's kitchen. She was a free-spirited spirit. She insisted on walking to the village, going where the men congregated, and conversing with them as equals. My mother thought the whole habit of women bowing to men was ridiculous. She didn't, however, refuse to do it. She went overboard. She made a farce of it. With this charming little curtsy, the other women would kneel before men. My mother would crawl down and cower, grovelling in the dirt as if she were worshipping a deity, and she'd stay there for a long time, like a very long period, long enough to make everyone uncomfortable. That was my mother. Don't go against the system. Make fun of the system. It appeared to Abel that his wife did not appreciate him. Every other man had some meek rural girl, and here he'd arrived with this modern woman, a Xhosa woman no less, from a culture whose women were supposed to be especially loudmouthed and promiscuous. My mother refused to return after the first trip since they argued and bickered the entire time.

I'd spent my entire life in a world governed by women, but once my mother and Abel married, and especially after Andrew was born, I witnessed him strive to express himself and impose his notions about what his family should be. Early on, it became evident that their ideas did not involve me. I reminded him that my mother had lived a life before him. I didn't even match his skin tone. His family consisted of him, my mother, and the new baby. My mother and I were my family. That was something I really liked about him. He was my buddy at times and not at others, but he never pretended our connection was anything other than what it was. We'd make up jokes and laugh together. We'd sit down to watch TV together. After my mother told him I'd had enough, he'd sneak me some pocket money. But he never gave me a gift for my birthday or Christmas. He never showed me the love of a parent. I was never his child.

With Abel's presence in the house came new restrictions. He kicked Fufi and Panther out of the house as one of the first things he did.

"No dogs allowed in the house."

"But we've always had dogs in the house."

"Not any longer. Outside of an African home, dogs slumber. Inside, people snooze."

Abel's decision to confine the dogs to the yard was his way of expressing, "We're going to do things around here the way they're supposed to be done." My mother was still a free spirit when they were dating, doing whatever she wanted and travelling wherever she wanted. Those things were gradually reined in. He seemed to be trying to limit our independence. He was even unhappy about church. "You can't stay at church all day," he'd say. "What will people say about my wife being gone all day?" 'Why isn't his wife present? What happened to her? Who spends the entire day in church?' No way, no how. This is disrespectful to me."

He attempted to get her to stop going to church so frequently, and one of the more effective methods he employed was to stop fixing my mother's car. It would break down, and he would purposely leave it alone. My mother couldn't afford another automobile and couldn't get the car repaired anywhere. You're married to a mechanic, and you're planning to have another technician fix your car? That is even worse than cheating. As a result, Abel became our sole mode of transportation, and he would refuse to take us anywhere. My mother, ever stubborn, would take minibuses to church.

Losing the car meant losing contact with my father. We had to ask Abel for rides into town, and he wasn't happy about it. It was a slap in the face to his manhood.

"We need to go to Yeoville."

"Why are you going to Yeoville?"

"To see Trevor's dad."

"What? No, no. How can I bring my wife and her child there and drop you off? You're making fun of me. What am I going to tell my friends? What should I say to my family? My wife is with another man? The man who fathered her child? No way, no how."

I was seeing my father less and less. Soon after, he relocated to Cape Town. Abel desired a conventional marriage with a conventional wife. For a long time, I questioned why he ever married someone like my mother in the first place, because she was the polar opposite in every way. If he wanted a woman to bow to him, there were plenty of girls being reared exclusively for that purpose in Tzaneen. According to my mother, a traditional man expects a woman to be subordinate, but he never falls in love with subservient women. He is drawn to strong-willed women. "He's like an exotic bird collector," she described him as. "He only wants a free woman because his dream is to imprison her."

Abel smoked a lot of pot when we first met him. He drank as well, but largely cannabis. In retrospect, I almost miss his pothead days since it mellowed him out. He'd smoke, relax, watch TV, and eventually fall asleep. I believe that was something he understood he needed to do unconsciously to calm down. He quit smoking after he married my mother. She forced him to stop for religious reasons—the body is a temple, after all. But what none of us expected was that when he quit consuming marijuana, he just replaced it with alcohol. He began to drink more and more. He never came home sober from work. A typical day included a six-pack of beer after work. He'd have a buzz on weeknights. He didn't come home on certain Fridays and Saturdays.

When Abel drank, his eyes turned crimson and bloodshot. That's how I learned to read. Abel has always struck me as a cobra: serene, completely still, then exploding. There was no yelling and raving, no fists clenched. He'd be quite quiet, and then the violence would appear out of nowhere. My single warning sign was the eyes. His eyes were everything to him. They were the Devil's eyes.

We awoke late one night to a smoke-filled house. By the time we'd gone to bed, Abel hadn't returned, and I'd fallen asleep in my mother's room with her and Andrew, who was still a baby. I startled awake as she shook me and screamed. "Trevor! Trevor! Trevor!" There was smoke in every direction. We believed the home was on fire.

My mother ran down the hall to the kitchen, where she discovered it on fire. Abel had returned home intoxicated, blind drunk, drunker than we'd ever seen him. He'd been hungry and attempted to heat up some food on the stove before passing out on the couch while it was cooking. The pot had blown up, destroying the kitchen wall behind the stove, and smoke was blowing everywhere. She turned off the stove and opened the doors and windows to let some fresh air in. Then she went over to the couch and woke him up, berating him for nearly burning down the house. He was too inebriated to care.

She returned to the bedroom, took up the phone, and dialled my grandmother's number. She started talking about Abel and his drinking. "This man is going to murder us one day." He almost burned down the house..."

Abel entered the bedroom calmly and quietly. His eyes were bright red, and his eyelids were thick. He hung up the phone with his finger on the cradle. My mother had a nervous breakdown. "How could you!?" Please do not disconnect my phone call! What on earth do you think you're doing?!"

"You don't tell people what's going on in this house," he explained.

"Please, please!" You're concerned about what the rest of the world is thinking? Be concerned about the state of the globe! Be concerned about what your family is thinking!"

My mother was dwarfed by Abel. He didn't get irritated or raise his voice.

"Mbuyi," he softly replied, "you don't respect me."

"Respect?! You nearly destroyed our home. Respect? Please, please! Earn your admiration! If you want me to respect you as a man, behave like one! Where are your child's diapers, and are you drinking your money in the streets? Respect?! Earn your admiration—"

"Mbuyi—"

"You're not even a man; you're a child—"

"Mbuyi—"

"I can't have a child for a husband—"

"Mbuyi—"

"I've got my own children to raise—"

"Mbuyi, please shut up—"

"A man who comes home drunk—" "Mbuyi, shut up—" "And then burns down his house with his children—"

"Mbuyi, please shut up—"

"And you're calling yourself a father—"

Then, like a thunderclap when there were no clouds, snap!, he hit her across the face. She ricocheted against the wall and crashed to the ground like a ton of bricks. It was unlike anything I'd ever seen. She fell and stayed down for around thirty seconds. Andrew began to scream. I don't recall going to pick him up, but I do recall holding him at some point. My mother struggled to her feet and launched herself right back into him. She'd clearly been thrown for a loop, but she was attempting to appear more composed than she was. Her face was filled with disbelief. Nothing like this had ever happened to her before. She went straight back in his face and began yelling at him.

"Did you really just hit me?"

I kept repeating to myself what Abel was saying the entire time. Stop talking, Mom. Stop talking. You're only going to make matters worse. Because I understood that, as a victim of numerous beatings, the one thing that doesn't help is yelling back. But she refused to be quiet.

"Did you really just hit me?"

"Mbuyi, as I told you—"

"No man ever has!" Don't think you can control me when you can't control yourself—"

Crack! He smacked her again. She stumbled back but did not fall this time. She scrambled, grabbed Andrew and me.

"All right, let's go. "We're departing."

We dashed out of the house and up the street. It was late at night and freezing outside. I was only wearing a T-shirt and sweatpants. We walked about a kilometre to the Eden Park police station. My mother led us in, and there were two cops stationed at the front desk.

"I'm here to lay the charge," she explained.

"What brings you here to lay a charge?"

"I'm here to file a complaint against the person who hit me."

I'll never forget how patronising and condescending they were to her.

"Slow down, lady. Please relax. "Who struck you?"

"My husband."

"Is he your husband?" What exactly did you do? "Did you irritate him?"

"Did I...what? No. He smacked me. I'm here to file a complaint against—"

"No, no. Ma'am. Why do you want to build a case? Are you certain you want to do this? Return home and speak with your hubby. You are aware that once charges are laid, they cannot be reversed? He will have a criminal history. His life will never be the same after this. "Do you really want your husband imprisoned?"

My mother insisted on taking a statement and opening a case, but they refused—they refused to type up a charge sheet.

"This is a family thing," they explained. "You don't want the cops involved." Maybe you should think about it and come back in the morning."

Mom began yelling at them, demanding to see the station commander, and Abel went into the station at the same time. He'd driven down there. He'd calmed down a little, but he was still inebriated when he drove into a police station. It didn't make a difference. He approached the cops, and the station was transformed into a guys' club. They appeared to be a group of longtime friends.

"Hey, guys," he introduced himself. "You already know how it is. You're aware of how women can be. "I was just a little irritated, that's all."

"It's fine, man. We are aware. It occurs. Don't be concerned."

I'd never seen anything like it before. I was nine years old, and I still saw the cops as good people. If you fall into difficulties, call the cops, and those flashing red and blue lights will come to your aid. But I remember standing there, stunned, shocked that these cops wouldn't aid my mother. That's when I understood the cops weren't who I had assumed they were. They were men first and police officers second.

We exited the station. My mother took Andrew and me to visit my grandma in Soweto for a few days. Abel drove by a few weeks later and apologised. Abel's apologies were usually genuine and heartfelt: he didn't mean it. He realises he was mistaken. He won't do that again. My grandmother persuaded my mum to give Abel another chance. Her main point was that "all men do it." Temperance, my grandfather, had hit her. It was no assurance that leaving Abel would prevent it from happening again, but at least Abel was willing to apologise. As a result, my mother decided to give him another chance. We drove back to Eden Park together, and nothing—for years, Abel didn't touch her. Or me. Everything was restored to its previous state. Abel was a fantastic mechanic, possibly the greatest around at the time. He attended technical school and graduated first in his class. BMW and Mercedes had both approached him with job offers. His company thrived on referrals. People would bring their cars from all across town for him to repair because he could perform miracles on them. My mother had complete faith in him. She hoped she could help him realise his full potential, not just as a mechanic but as the owner of his own workshop.

My mother, as powerful and independent as she is, is the woman who gives back. It's in her nature to give and give and give. At home, she refused to be obedient to Abel, but she did want him to succeed as a man. If she could make their marriage a true marriage of equals, she was willing to devote herself totally into it, just as she did her children. Abel's boss eventually chose to sell Mighty Mechanics and retire. My mother had some money saved up and assisted Abel in purchasing it. They relocated the workshop from Yeoville to Wynberg, just west of Alex, and Mighty Mechanics became the new family business.

Nobody tells you everything when you initially start a business. That's especially true when you're two young black people, a secretary and a mechanic, who grew up in a time when blacks were not allowed to own any enterprises at all. Nobody informs you that when you acquire a firm, you also buy its debt. When my mother and Abel opened the Mighty Mechanics books and realised what they'd purchased, they recognized how much trouble the company was already in.

Our lives were progressively taken over by the garage. I'd leave school and go the five kilometres to the workshop from Maryvale. I'd sit for hours, trying to finish my homework as machinery and repairs ran around me. Abel would always be late on a car, and since he was our ride, we'd have to wait for him to complete before we could go home. "We're running late," it began. Go take a nap in the van, and we'll let you know when we're leaving." I'd slide into the backseat of a sedan, they'd wake me up around midnight, and we'd go back to Eden Park and crash. Soon after, it was "We're running late." We'll wake you up for school in the morning if you sleep in the van." We began sleeping in the garage. It started with one or two nights per week, then three or four. My mother then sold the house and invested the proceeds in the business. She put everything on the line. She sacrificed everything for him.

We lived in the garage from then on. It was a warehouse, but not the elegant, romantic kind that hipsters could one day renovate into lofts. No, no. It was a freezing, empty space. Grey concrete flooring soiled with oil and grease, old junk automobiles and car components strewn about. There was a tiny office erected out of drywall towards the front, next to the roller door that opened onto the street, for documents and such. A kitchenette was located at the back, consisting of a sink, a portable hot plate, and several cabinets. There was only an open wash basin, similar to a janitor's sink, with a showerhead put up above to bathe in.

Abel and my mother shared Andrew's office bed, which was a tiny mattress rolled out on the floor. In the automobiles, I slept. I became rather adept at sleeping in cars. I'm familiar with the best autos for sleeping in. The worst were the low-end Japanese sedans and Volkswagens. The chairs were barely reclined, there were no headrests, and the fabric was terrible faux leather. I'd spend most of the night trying not to fall out of my seat. I'd wake up with painful knees from not being able to stretch and extend my legs. German automobiles, particularly Mercedes, were fantastic. Large, luxurious leather seats, similar to couches. They were cold when you first entered, but they were well insulated and quickly warmed up. I only needed my school blazer to wrap up under to get incredibly warm inside a Mercedes. The best, hands down, were American automobiles. I used to wish for a customer to arrive in a large Buick with bench seats. If I saw one of those, I'd say, "Yes!" It was unusual for American cars to arrive, but when they did, I was in heaven.

I had to work since Mighty Mechanics was now a family business, and I was family. There was no more time to have fun. There was no time for schoolwork at all. I'd walk home, take off my school uniform, put on my overalls, and climb under the hood of some sedan. I eventually got to the point where I could conduct basic car maintenance on my own, which I frequently did. "That Honda," Abel would say. "Minor duty." I'd also get beneath the hood. Every single day. Points, plugs, condensers, oil filters, and air filters are all examples of components. Install new seats, replace tires, exchange headlights, and repair tail lights. Go to the parts store, buy the parts, and then return to the workshop. That was my life when I was eleven years old. I was slipping behind in class. I wasn't accomplishing anything. My teachers used to be harsh with me.

"Why aren't you doing your homework?"

"I'm unable to complete my homework." I have jobs to do at home."

We worked and worked and worked, but the business remained losing money no matter how many hours we put in. We had everything destroyed. We couldn't even afford fresh produce. There was one month in particular that I'll never forget, the worst month of my life. We were so poor that we lived on bowls of marogo, a type of wild spinach boiled with caterpillars, for weeks. They're known as mopane worms. Mopane worms are simply the cheapest thing on the planet, eaten only by the poorest of the poor. I grew up poor, but poverty isn't the same as "Wait, I'm eating worms." Mopane worms are the kind of item that would make even Soweto residents say, "Eh...no." They're the size of your finger, these spiky, vividly coloured caterpillars. They're not like escargot, where someone gave a snail a nice name. They're filthy worms. As you consume them, their black spines stab the roof of your mouth. When you bite into a mopane worm, its yellow-green faeces may squirt into your mouth.

I kind of liked the caterpillars for a time. It was like a gastronomic adventure at first, but after a few weeks of eating them every day, day after day, I couldn't handle it any more. I'll never forget the time I bit a mopane worm in half and that yellow-green goo oozed out, and I thought to myself, "I'm eating caterpillar shit." I felt like puking right away. I lost it and fled to my mother, crying. "I don't want to eat caterpillars anymore!" That night, she pulled together some money and purchased us chicken. We'd never gone without food before, no matter how impoverished we were.

Work all night, sleep in some car, wake up, wash up in a janitor's sink, brush my teeth in a little metal basin, brush my hair in the rearview mirror of a Toyota, then try to get dressed without getting oil and grease all over my school clothes so the kids don't know I live in a garage. Oh, how I despised it. I detested automobiles. I despised sleeping in automobiles. I despised working on automobiles. I despised getting my hands filthy. I detested eating worms. I despised everything.

Surprisingly, I didn't despise my mother or even Abel. Because I witnessed how hard everyone worked. At first, I was unaware of the business flaws that were making things difficult, so it just felt like a difficult scenario. But, ultimately, I realised why the company was losing money. I used to travel around buying auto parts for Abel, and I discovered that he was doing so on credit. The sellers were charging him exorbitant prices. The debt was strangling the company, and instead of paying it off, he was drinking his little earnings. Excellent mechanic, dreadful salesman.

To try to salvage the garage, my mother quit her job at ICI and stepped in to assist him in running the business. She carried her office talents to the garage and began managing the books, making the timetable, and balancing the accounts full-time. And everything was going swimmingly until Abel began to suspect that she was controlling his company. People began to comment on it as well. Clients received their vehicles on time, vendors were paid on time, and they would comment, "Hey, Abie, this workshop is going so much better now that your wife has taken over." That didn't help matters.

We lived in the workshop for over a year before my mother had had enough. She was eager to assist him, but only provided he drank all of the proceeds. She'd always been self-sufficient and independent, but she'd lost that part of herself at the whim of someone else's shattered dream. "I can't do this anymore," she stated at one point. I'm out of here. "I'm finished." She went out and obtained a job as a secretary for a real-estate developer, and she was able to get us the house in Highlands North by borrowing against whatever equity was left in Abel's workshop. We relocated, Abel's creditors took the workshop, and that was the end of that.

Growing up, I was subjected to a lot of my mother's old-school, Old Testament discipline. She spared no child and spared no rod. She was different from Andrew. He was spanked at first, but they gradually decreased and then stopped. When I asked her why I was getting beaten up while Andrew wasn't, she made a joke about it, as she does with everything. "I beat you like that because I knew you could take it," she explained. "I can't hit your younger brother as hard because he's a skinny little stick." He'll snap. God, on the other hand, gave you that ass for whipping." Even though she was joking, I could tell she didn't beat Andrew because she'd had a true change of heart about it. She'd learnt it from me, strangely enough.

I grew up in a violent world, yet I was never violent myself. I did pull pranks, set fires, and break windows, but I never harmed individuals. I have never hit someone. I was never upset. I just didn't view myself in that light. My mother had shown me a different world than the one she had grown up in. She gave me the books she never got around to reading. She took me to schools she never got to attend. I immersed myself in those worlds and returned with a new perspective on the world. Not all households are violent, as I discovered. I observed the futility of violence, the never-ending cycle, the harm done on people, which they in turn inflict on others.

More than anything, I saw that relationships are preserved by love rather than violence. Love is an act of creation. When you fall in love with someone, you construct a new world for them. That was done for me by my mother, and with the progress I made and the things I learned, I returned and established a new world and a new understanding for her. She never lifted her hand to her children again after that. Unfortunately, by the time she came to a halt, Abel had already begun.

I was never afraid of my mother, even when she was beating me. I surely didn't enjoy it. "I hit you out of love," she continued, and I didn't necessarily agree with her reasoning. But I realised it was discipline, and it was done for a reason. I felt something I'd never felt before the first time Abel punched me. I was terrified.

I was in sixth grade, my final year at Maryvale. We'd relocated to Highlands North, and I'd gotten in trouble at school for faking my mother's signature on some document; there was some activity I didn't want to be a part of, so I'd signed the release in her name to avoid it. My mother was contacted by the school, and she inquired about it when I returned home that afternoon. I was certain she would punish me, but this turned out to be one of those occasions when she didn't care. She stated that I should have simply asked her; she would have signed the form regardless. Then Abel, who had been sitting in the kitchen with us, asked, "Hey, can I talk to you for a second?" Then he led me into this small space, a walk-in pantry off the kitchen, and shut the door behind us.

He was standing between me and the door, but I didn't notice. It never occurred to me to be afraid. Abel had never previously attempted to reprimand me. He'd never even lectured me before. "Mbuyi, your son did this," my mother would always say, and then she would address it. It was also the middle of the afternoon. He was absolutely sober, which added to the terror of what transpired next.

"Why did you forge your mother's signature?" he wondered.

I began making up an excuse. "Oh, I, uh, I forgot to bring the form home—"

"Don't tell me anything. "How come you forged your mother's signature?"

I began stuttering more nonsense, clueless to what was about to happen, and suddenly it appeared out of nowhere.

The first blow landed in my ribs. My thoughts raced: It's a trap! I'd never been in a fight before, and I'd never learned how to fight, but something prompted me to get in close. I'd seen what those lengthy arms were capable of. I'd watched him kill my mother, but more importantly, I'd seen him kill grown men. Abel never punched anyone; I never witnessed him punch someone with a closed fist. But he could hit a grown guy across the face with an open palm and make him crumple. He was that powerful. When I saw his arms, I knew I didn't want to be on the receiving end of those things. I ducked in close, and he continued to hit, but I was too close for him to land any serious blows. Then he realised what was going on and stopped beating me and began grappling and wrestling me. He did this thing where he gripped the skin on my arms between his thumb and forefinger and twisted hard. That stung, Jesus.

It was the most horrifying experience I'd ever had. I'd never been that terrified before. Because it served no purpose—that's what made it so terrible. It wasn't a matter of discipline. Nothing about it was coming from a loving place. It didn't feel like it was going to end with me learning a lesson about forging my mother's signature. It felt like it would finish when he wanted it to, when his wrath had worn off. It felt as if something within him desired to destroy me. Abel was bigger and stronger than me, but being in such a small place worked in my favour because he didn't have much room to manoeuvre. I managed to twist and wiggle my way around him and out the door while he wrestled and pummelling. I was quick, but Abel was also swift. He pursued me. I dashed out of the house, hopped over the gate, and ran, ran, ran. He was rounding the gate, coming out of the yard after me the last time I turned around. I had recurring nightmares about the look on his face as he came around the corner until I was twenty-five years old.

I dropped my head and ran as soon as I spotted him. I ran as if the Devil was after me. Although Abel was bigger and faster, this was my neighbourhood. You wouldn't be able to catch me in my neighbourhood. I knew every alley and street, every wall to scale, and every fence to breach. I was avoiding traffic and cutting across yards. I'm not sure when he finally gave up because I never glanced back. I ran and ran and ran till my legs gave out. I was in Bramley, three neighbourhoods away, when I came to a halt. I crept into some bushes, crawled inside, and crouched there for what felt like hours.

You don't have to teach me the same thing twice. I stayed in that house like a mouse from that day till the day I left. I was out of a room if Abel was in there. He was in one corner, and I was in the other. If he entered a room, I would get up and pretend to go to the kitchen, then when I returned, I would make sure I was close to the exit. He may be in the most upbeat, friendly attitude. It didn't make a difference. I never let him get between me and a door again. Maybe a handful of times after that when I was sloppy and he'd land a punch or a kick before I could get away, but I never trusted him again.

Andrew's experience was unique. Abel's kid, flesh of his flesh and blood of his blood. Despite being nine years younger than me, Andrew was the eldest son in that family, Abel's firstborn, and he was treated with respect that neither I nor my mother had. Despite his flaws, Andrew had nothing but admiration for that man. Andrew, I believe, was the only one who wasn't terrified because of that love. He was the lion tamer, but he'd been raised by the lion, and while knowing what the beast was capable of, he couldn't love it any less. For me, Abel's first gleam of rage or insanity was gone. Andrew would stay and try to reason with Abel. He'd even get in the way of Abel and Mom. I recall Abel hurling a bottle of Jack Daniel's at Andrew's head one night. It narrowly avoided him and burst against the wall. That is, Andrew stayed long enough to have the bottle thrown at him. I wouldn't have stayed long enough for Abel to have a good look at me.

Abel had to get his cars out when Mighty Mechanics went bankrupt. Someone was seizing the property, and there were liens on his assets. It was a shambles. That's when he began operating his workshop out of our backyard. It was also the year my mother divorced him.

There are two types of marriage in African culture: legal marriage and traditional marriage. Just because you formally divorce someone does not imply they are no longer your spouse. When Abel's debts and poor business decisions began to affect my mother's credit and capacity to maintain her sons, she wanted out. "I don't have any debts," she explained. "I don't have a bad credit history." These things are not happening with you." We were still a family, and they were still married in the formal sense, but she divorced him to separate their financial issues. She also changed her name.

Because Abel had begun operating an unlicensed business in a residential area, one of our neighbours filed a petition to have us removed. My mother applied for a business licence so that she could run a business on the property. The workshop remained, but Abel continued to run it into the ground, drinking his money. At the same time, my mother began to advance in her position at the real estate firm where she worked, taking on more duties and earning a higher salary. His craft had nearly become a side pastime for him. He was supposed to pay Andrew's school fees and food, but he fell behind on even those, and my mother soon had to pay for everything. She had to pay for the electricity. She completed the mortgage payment. He literally made no contribution.

That was the watershed moment. When my mother started making more money and regaining her independence, we saw the dragon appear. The drinking became worse. He became increasingly violent. Abel beat my mother for the second time not long after coming for me in the pantry. I can't remember the specifics since it's now mixed with all the other instances that came after it. I recall that the cops were called. They came out to the house again, but this time it was like a boys' club. "Hello, folks. You know how these women are." There was no report. There were no charges filed.

Whenever he assaulted her or chased me, my mother would find me crying and take me aside. She'd always give me the same speech.

"Pray for Abel," she'd tell you. "Because he doesn't despise us." He despises himself."

This makes no sense to a child. "Well, if he hates himself," I'd argue, "why doesn't he kick himself?"

Abel was one of those drinkers who, after he was gone, you couldn't even see the same person in his eyes. I recall him coming home intoxicated and stumbling through the house one night. He stumbled into my room, muttering to himself, and when I awoke, he had pulled out his dick and was pissing on the floor. He mistook himself for being in the restroom. He'd get so intoxicated that he wouldn't recognize which room of the home he was in. He would come into my room thinking it was his, kick me out of bed, and pass out on numerous occasions. I'd holler at him, but it felt like I was speaking to a zombie. I'd crash on the couch.

Every evening after work, he'd get intoxicated with his crew in the backyard, and many evenings he'd wind up fighting with one of them. Someone would say something that irritated Abel, and he'd beat the crap out of them. The guy wouldn't show up for work on Tuesdays or Wednesdays, but he'd be back by Thursday because he needed the money. It was the same tale every few weeks, like clockwork.

Abel also kicked the dogs. Mostly Fufi. Panther was wise enough to stay away, while Fufi was always attempting to be Abel's friend. When he'd had a few, she'd cross his path or get in his way, and he'd give her the boot. She'd then go hide elsewhere for a time. Fufi getting booted was always an indication that something bad was about to happen. The dogs and employees in the yard typically got the first taste of his rage, alerting the rest of us to stay quiet. I'd generally go locate Fufi and stay with her wherever she was.

The funny thing was that Fufi never yelped or wailed when she was booted. When the vet discovered she was deaf, he also discovered she had a condition in which she didn't have a fully developed sense of touch. She was not in any discomfort. That's why she'd constantly start again with Abel as if it were a fresh day. He'd kick her, she'd run away, just to return the next morning, tail wagging. "Hey. I've arrived. I'll give you a second opportunity."

And he was always given a second opportunity. The pleasant and charming Abel never vanished. He was a lovely person with a drinking problem. We were a family. Growing up in an abusive home, you battle with the idea that you may love someone you despise or despise someone you love. It's an odd sensation. You wish to live in a world where people are either good or bad, where you either hate or adore them, but that is not the case.

There was an underlying sense of fear throughout the house, although the beatings themselves were not regular. If they had been, I believe the incident would have ended sooner. The nice times in between, ironically, were what allowed it to stretch on and escalate as far as it went. He hit my mother once, then again three years later, and this time it was even worse. Then it was two years later, and things had gotten a little worse. Then it was a year later, and things had gotten a little worse. It was sporadic enough that you'd assume it wouldn't happen again, but often enough that you never forgot it could. It had a beat to it. Nobody spoke to him for over a month after one particularly heinous episode. Nothing, no words, no eye contact, no talks. At different moments, we moved through the house as strangers. The silent treatment is complete. Then one morning in the kitchen, you hear a nod. "Hey." "Hey." Then it's "Did you see the thing on the news?" a week later. "Yeah." The following week, there is a joke and a laugh. Slowly, slowly, life returns to normal. Six months, a year later, you repeat the process.

My mother was unhappy and worked up when I arrived home from Sandringham one afternoon.

"This man is unbelievable," she said.

"What happened?"

"He bought a gun."

"What? A gun? "What do you mean, 'He purchased a gun?'"

A gun was such a silly item in my perspective. Only cops and criminals had guns in my mind. Abel had gone out and purchased a 9mm Parabellum Smith & Wesson. Sleek and dark, intimidating. It didn't seem cool like guns in movies. It appeared to be capable of killing things.

"Why did he buy a gun?" I enquired.

"I don't know."

She claimed she questioned him about it, and he went off on some gibberish about the world needing to learn to appreciate him.

"He thinks he's the world's policeman," she explained. "And that is the world's problem." We have people who can't police themselves, so they want to police everyone else."

I left not long after that. For me, the environment had turned toxic. I'd grown to the size of Abel. Big enough to fight back. A father does not fear retaliation from his son, but I was not his son. He was well aware of it. My mother made the analogy that there were now two male lions in the house. "Every time he looks at you, he sees your father," she'd remark. "You're a constant reminder of another man." You must depart because he despises you. You must leave before you become like him."

It was also past time for me to leave. Regardless of Abel, our goal had always been for me to move out after school. My mother never wanted me to be like my uncle, who was unemployed and still lived at home with his mother. She assisted me in obtaining my apartment, and I relocated. The flat was only ten minutes away from the house, so I was always available to help with errands or to have supper once in a while. But, most importantly, whatever was going on with Abel, I didn't have to be a part of it.

My mother eventually moved to a separate bedroom in the house, and from then on they were married in name only, not even cohabiting but coexisting. That state of affairs lasted a year, maybe two. Andrew had turned nine, and in my mind, I was counting down the days until he turned eighteen, thinking it would finally rescue my mother from this horrible man. Then, one afternoon, my mother called and asked me to come by the house. I dropped by a couple hours later.

"Trevor," she said. "I'm pregnant."

"Sorry, what?"

"I'm pregnant."

"What?!"

I was enraged. I was enraged. She seemed resolute, as determined as ever, but with an undertone of sadness I'd never seen before, as if the news had devastated her at first but she'd since reconciled herself to the truth of it.

"How could you have let this happen?"

"Abel and I made this up. I went back into my bedroom. It was only one night, and then...I became pregnant. I'm not sure how."

She didn't know. She was forty-four years old. She'd had her tubes tied after Andrew. "This shouldn't be possible," her doctor had remarked. "We have no idea how this happened."

I was enraged. All we had to do was wait for Andrew to mature and it would be finished, and now it was as if she'd renewed the contract.

"So you're going to have this child with this man?" You're going to stay with this man for another eighteen years? "Are you crazy?"

"God spoke to me, Trevor," he said. 'Patricia, I don't do anything by accident,' he said. Nothing I give you will be too much for you.' There's a reason I'm pregnant. I know what kind of children I can produce. I know what kind of sons I'm capable of raising. I am capable of raising this child. This child will be raised by me."

Isaac was born nine months later. She named him Isaac because in the Bible, Sarah becomes pregnant at the age of a hundred and is not supposed to have children, so she calls her baby Isaac.

Isaac's birth distanced me much more. I was visiting less and less. Then I came by one afternoon and found the house in disarray, with police cars out front, the aftermath of another brawl.

He'd smacked her with a bicycle. My mother had tried to intervene when Abel was berating one of his workers in the yard. Abel was enraged because she had contradicted him in front of an employee, so he grabbed Andrew's bike and beat her with it. She contacted the cops again, and this time the officers who arrived knew Abel. He'd serviced their vehicles. They were friends. There were no charges filed. There was no action.

I confronted him at the moment. I was finally large enough.

"You can't keep doing this," I told her. "This cannot be right."

He expressed regret. He always was. He didn't push out his chest or get defensive in any way.

"I know," he admitted. "I apologise. I dislike doing these things, but you know your mother. She has a lot to say yet she doesn't listen. Sometimes I feel like your mother doesn't respect me. She came in and insulted me in front of my employees. I can't have these other men staring at me as if I'm incapable of controlling my wife."

After the bicycle, my mother hired real-estate contractors she knew to build her a separate house in the backyard, sort of like a servants' quarters, and she moved in with Isaac.

"This is the most insane thing I've ever seen," I exclaimed to her.

"This is all I can do," she admitted. "The cops aren't going to help me. The government will not defend me. Only my God can keep me safe. But what I can do is use the one thing he values most against him: his pride. Everyone will ask him, 'Why does your wife live in a shanty outside your house?' because I dwell outside in a shack. He'll have to answer that question, and no matter what he says, everyone will realise there's something wrong with him. He enjoys living for the sake of the planet. Allow the rest of the world to see him for who he is. In the streets, he's a saint. In this house, he's the devil. Allow him to be recognized for what he is."

I was on the verge of dismissing my mother when she decided to retain Isaac. I couldn't take the torture any longer. But witnessing her struck with a bicycle and living like a prisoner in her own backyard was the final straw. I was a shattered individual. I was finished.

"This thing?" I asked. "What is this dysfunctional thing?" I'm not going to be a part of it. I can't go through life with you. I decline. You've made your choice. Best wishes in your life. "I'm going to live my own life."

She was aware. She had no sense of being betrayed or abandoned.

"Honey, I know exactly what you're going through," she remarked. "At one point, I had to disown my family in order to live my own life." I understand why you feel compelled to do the same."

As a result, I did. I walked away. I didn't make a phone call. I did not go. Isaac arrived and I went, and I couldn't figure out why she wouldn't do the same: leave. Simply leave. Simply fuck off.

I had no idea what she was going through. I had no idea what domestic violence was. I had no idea how adult relationships worked; I'd never had a girlfriend. I couldn't understand how she could have sex with someone she despised and despised. I had no idea how readily sex, hatred, and terror could collide.

I was furious at my mother. I despised him, but blamed her. I saw Abel as a decision she'd made, and one she was still making. "You cannot blame anyone else for what you do," she had always said to me throughout my childhood as she told me stories about growing up in the homelands and being abandoned by her parents. You cannot blame your present self on your history. You are only responsible for yourself. You make your own decisions."

She never let me perceive us as helpless victims. My mother and I, as well as Andrew and Isaac, were victims. Affirmative action victims. Abuse victims. But I was never permitted to think that way, and I never saw her life in that light. She chose to remove my father from our life in order to appease Abel. Her decision was to support Abel's workshop. Isaac was her selection. He didn't have the money; she did. She was not reliant. In my mind, she was the one who made the decision.

From the outside, it's so simple to blame the woman and say, "You just need to leave." It's not like my family was the only one that experienced domestic violence. It's what I grew up with. It was on the streets of Soweto, on TV, and in movies. In a culture where this is the standard, where does a woman go? When the cops refuse to assist her? When her own family refuses to assist her? Where does a woman go after leaving one man who strikes her and is equally likely to end up with another man who hits her, possibly much worse than the first? Where does a lady go when she is unmarried with three children and lives in a culture that regards her as a pariah because she is a manless woman? Where is she considered a whore for doing so? What happens to her? What exactly does she do?

But I didn't understand any of it at the time. I was a boy with a boy's perspective on things. I recall the previous time we argued over it as well. It was either after the bicycle or while she was moving into her garden shack. I was leaving, pleading with her for the thousandth time.

"Why? "Why don't you just go?"

She made a shaky motion with her head. "Oh, my baby. No way, no how. I'm unable to leave."

"Why not?" says one.

"Because if I don't leave, he'll kill us."

She wasn't being overly theatrical. She kept her voice down. I never asked her that question again because she answered it so calmly and matter-of-factly.

She did eventually leave. I have no idea what led her to leave or what the last breaking point was. I had left. I was on my way to become a comedian, touring the country, performing in England, presenting radio shows, and hosting television shows. I'd moved in with my cousin Mlungisi and separated my life from hers. I couldn't invest myself any longer because it would have broken me up too much. But then she relocated to Highlands North, met someone new, and moved on with her life. Andrew and Isaac still saw their father, who was just existing in the world at that point, still going through the same cycle of drinking and fighting, still living in a house paid for by his ex-wife.

Years have passed. Life went on.

Then, about ten a.m., I was in bed when my phone called. It happened on a Sunday. I knew it was a Sunday because everyone else in the family had gone to church and I had not. My days of continually schlepping back and forth to church were over, and I was now sleeping in. The irony of my life is that whenever church is involved, bad things happen, such as being kidnapped by violent minibus drivers. I'd often mocked my mother about it. "What good has your church, all this Jesus, brought you?"

I took a look at my phone. It displayed my mother's phone number, but when I responded, it was Andrew on the other end. He sounded completely at ease.

"Hello, Trevor, this is Andrew."

"Hey."

"How are things going for you?"

"Good. "How are you?"

"Are you very busy?"

"I'm kind of sleeping." Why?"

"Mom's been shot."

So, there were two odd things about the call. First and foremost, why would he inquire whether I was busy? Let's begin there. When your mother is shot, the first thing you should say is "Mom's been shot." "How are you?" does not suffice. "Are you too busy?" That perplexed me. The second strange thing was that when he said, "Mom's been shot," I didn't immediately question, "Who shot her?" I wasn't required to. "Mom's been shot," he added, and my mind immediately filled in the rest: "Abel shot mom."

"Where are you right now?" I said.

"We're currently at Linksfield Hospital."

"Okay, I'm on my way."

I leapt out of bed and dashed down the corridor, banging on Mlungisi's door. "Dude, my mom was shot!" She's been admitted to the hospital." He leaped out of bed as well, and we rushed to the hospital, which was just fifteen minutes away.

I was upset but not afraid at the time. Andrew had been so calm on the phone, no crying, no terror in his voice, that I assumed she was well. It can't be that horrible. I contacted him again from the car to learn more.

"Andrew, can you tell me what happened?"

"We were on our way home from church," he explained calmly. "And Dad was there waiting for us at the house, and he got out of his car and started shooting."

"However, where?" "Did he shoot her?"

"He fired a shot into her leg."

"Oh, okay," I answered.

"And then he shot her in the back of the head."

My body just let go when he said that. I recall precisely which traffic light I was at. There was a perfect silence for a time, and then I cried like I'd never cried before. I slumped, sobbing and moaning. I cried as if every other thing I'd ever cried over had been a waste of tears. If my current weeping self could go back in time and see my previous crying selves, it would slap them and say, "That shit's not worth crying for." My son was not one of grief. It was not a cathartic experience. It wasn't because I was feeling sorry for myself. It was an expression of raw pain caused by my body's incapacity to communicate that pain in any other way, shape, or form. She was my mother. She was a member of my team. It had always been just me and her, us against the world. When Andrew said, "shot her in the head," I split in half.

The light shifted. I couldn't see the road, but I drove through the tears, telling myself, "Just get there, just get there, just get there." When we arrived at the hospital, I jumped out of the car. There was an outdoor seating area near the emergency room entrance. Andrew stood alone, his clothes stained with blood, waiting for me. He still appeared perfectly calm and stoic. Then, as soon as he spotted me, he broke down and began sobbing. It was as though he'd been holding it together all morning and then everything came crashing down on him all at once. I hurried up to him and held him, and he sobbed uncontrollably. His wail, though, was not the same as mine. My cries were filled with agony and rage. His cries were of helplessness.

I turned around and dashed into the emergency department. My mother was on a gurney in triage. Her condition was being stabilised by the doctors. Her entire body was covered with blood. There was a hole in her face, a huge incision above her lip, and a chunk of her nose was missing.

She was as placid and calm as I'd ever seen her. She could still open one eye, and she turned to look up at me, seeing the terror on my face.

"It's okay, baby," she said quietly, barely able to speak because of the blood in her throat.

"It's not okay."

"No, no, I'm fine, I'm fine." What happened to Andrew? "Where has your brother gone?"

"He's gone outside."

"Go talk to Andrew."

"But, Mom—"

"Shh. It's all right, baby. "I'm all right."

"You're not fine, you're—"

"Shhh. I'm okay, I'm okay, I'm okay. Visit your brother. Your sibling requires your assistance."

The physicians continued to work, and there was nothing I could do to assist her. I returned outside to see Andrew. He sat down with me and told me the story.

They were returning from church in a large group, my mother and Andrew and Isaac, her new husband and his children, as well as a large number of his extended family, aunts and uncles, nieces and nephews. When Abel arrived and got out of his car, they had just pulled into the driveway. He was armed. He locked his gaze on my mother.

"You've stolen my life," he declared. "You've stripped everything from me. Now I'm going to kill you all."

Andrew took a step in front of his father. He took a step right in front of the cannon.

"Please don't do this, Dad. You're inebriated. Simply put the pistol away."

Abel lowered his gaze to his son.

"No," he replied. "I'm going to kill everyone, and if you don't leave, I'll shoot you first."

Andrew took a step back.

"His eyes were not lying," he said. "He had the Devil's eyes." "I knew my father was gone at that moment."

In retrospect, for all the sorrow I felt that day, I have to think Andrew's pain was considerably worse than mine. My mother had been murdered by a guy I detested. I felt vindicated; I'd been correct about Abel all along. I could direct my rage and fury towards him without feeling any shame or guilt. But Andrew's mother had been murdered by Andrew's father, whom he adored. How can he reconcile his love with the circumstances? How does he continue to love both sides? Both aspects of himself?

Isaac was only four years old at the time. Isaac began crying as Andrew stood aside, not completely understanding what was going on.

"What are you doing, Daddy?" "What are you doing, Daddy?"

"Isaac, please go to your brother," Abel instructed.

Andrew grabbed Isaac as he ran over to him. Abel then raised his revolver and began shooting. To protect everyone, my mother jumped in front of the gun, and that's when she got the first bullet, not in her leg but in her butt cheek. She crumpled and screamed as she fell to the ground.

"Run!"

Abel continued to shoot, and everyone fled. They dispersed. When Abel approached and stood over my mother, she was struggling to get back to her feet. He pointed the gun at her head, like an executioner. Then he fired the shot. Nothing. The rifle accidentally discharged. Click! He pulled the trigger again, and the same thing happened. Then it happened again and again. Click, click, click, click, click! He pushed the trigger four times, and each time the gun misfired. Bullets were ejecting from the ejection port, falling from the pistol, landing on my mother and clattering to the ground.

Abel came to a halt to inspect the rifle. My mum leapt up in fright. She pushed him aside, dashed to her car, and leapt into the driver's seat. Andrew dashed behind her and jumped into the passenger seat beside her. Andrew heard one last gunshot as she cranked the ignition, and the windshield glowed red. Abel had opened fire from behind the vehicle. The gunshot entered her head and exited through the front of her face, splattering blood everywhere. Her shoulders sagged over the steering wheel. Andrew yanked my mother to the passenger seat, threw her over, leaped into the driver's seat, pushed the car into gear, and sped to the hospital in Linksfield.

I inquired as to what had happened to Abel. He had no idea. I was enraged, but there was nothing I could do. I felt absolutely powerless, but I felt compelled to act. So I got out my phone and dialled his number—the man who had just shot my mother—and he genuinely answered.

"Trevor."

"You killed my mom."

"Yes, I did."

"You killed my mom!"

"Yes. And if I could find you, I'd kill you too."

He then hung up. It was the most terrifying scene. It was frightening. I quickly lost the courage I'd mustered to call him. I'm still not sure what I was thinking. I'm not sure what I expected to happen. I was simply outraged.

I kept asking Andrew questions, hoping to elicit additional information. A nurse came outside seeking for me while we were conversing.

"Are you part of the family?" she inquired.

"Yes."

"Sir, there is an issue. At first, your mother said a little. She's now quit, but we've learned she doesn't have health insurance."

"What? No, no. That can't be right. "I believe my mother has health insurance."

She didn't do it. As it turned out, she'd determined a few months before, "This health insurance is a scam." I'm never sick. I'm calling it off." As a result, she no longer had health insurance.

"We can't treat your mother here," explained the nurse. "If she doesn't have insurance, we'll have to send her to a state hospital."

"Another state hospital?" What—no! You simply cannot. My mother was shot in the head. You're putting her back on a gurney? Should we send her out in an ambulance? She'll perish. You must treat her straight away."

"We can't, Sir. We require a method of payment."

"I'm your payment method." "I will pay."

"Yes, people say that, but without any guarantee—"

I took out my credit card.

"Here," I explained. "Here, take this. I'll cover the cost. "I'll cover everything."

"Sir, hospitalisation can be very expensive."

"I don't really care."

"I don't think you understand, Sir." Hospitalisation can be very costly."

"Lady, I have some money." I'll pay whatever it takes. Just assist us."

"You don't understand, Sir. We have a lot of tests to run. A single test could cost two or three thousand rand."

"Three trillion—what? Lady, we're talking about my mother's life here. "I will pay."

"You don't understand, Sir. Your mother was shot. In her head. She'll be in intensive care. One night in the ICU might cost you between 15,000 and 20,000 rand."

"Lady, are you not paying attention to me?" This is the story of my mother's life. This is her existence. Take the cash. Take everything. "I don't mind."

"Sir! You don't get it. This has happened to me. Your mother could remain in the intensive care unit for several weeks. This might cost you between $500,000 and $6,000,000. Possibly millions. You're going to be in debt for the rest of your life."

I'm not going to lie to you: I took a breather. I took a long pause. At that point, I heard the nurse say, "All of your money will be gone," and I began to think, Well...what is she, fifty? That's quite good, isn't it? She has had a lovely life.

I honestly didn't know what to do. I looked at the nurse, stunned by what she'd stated. My thoughts raced through a slew of alternative situations. What if I spend the money and she still dies? Do I receive a refund? I pictured my frugal mother coming up from a sleep and asking, "How much did you spend?" You moron. You should've saved that money to help your brothers." How about my brothers? They would suddenly be my responsibility. I'd have to raise the family, which I couldn't do if I was in debt to the tune of millions of dollars, and it was always my mother's solemn promise that raising my brothers was the one thing I'd never have to do. Even as my career took off, she turned down any assistance I offered. "I don't want you paying for your mother in the same way that I had to pay for mine," she'd say. "I don't want you raising your brothers in the same way that Abel had to raise his."

My mother's greatest concern was that I would wind up paying the black tax, caught in the cycle of poverty and violence that had come before me. She had always said I would be the one to break the cycle. I'd be the one to move forward rather than back. And as I stood outside the emergency hospital, I was terrified that the moment I handed her my credit card, the cycle would resume and I'd be dragged back in.

People frequently state that they would do anything for the people they care about. But would you really do it? What would you do? Would you give it all? I don't think a child understands that type of altruistic love. Yes, a mother. A mother will hold her children and leap from a moving car to protect them. She will do it without hesitation. But I doubt the child knows how to do it automatically. It is something that the child must learn.

I placed my credit card in the nurse's grasp.

"Do whatever needs to be done. Please assist my mother."

We spent the remainder of the day in limbo, waiting, not knowing, walking about the hospital, and being visited by family members. After several hours, the doctor finally emerged from the emergency department to give us an update.

"What's happening?" I inquired.

"Your mother is stable," he assured her. "She's out of surgery."

"Is she going to be okay?"

He paused for a bit to consider what he was about to say.

"I don't like to use this word," he explained, "because I'm a scientist and don't believe in it." But what happened to your mother today was nothing short of miraculous. I never say that because I despise it when people do, but I don't know how else to describe this."

He claimed that the bullet that impacted my mother in the buttocks was a through-and-through. It went in, came out, and did no serious harm. The other bullet entered below the skull at the top of her neck into the back of her head. It narrowly avoided the spinal cord, the medulla oblongata, and passed through her head just beneath the brain, missing every major vein, artery, and nerve. The bullet was on a trajectory that would have blown out her left eye socket, but at the last second it slowed down, hit her cheekbone instead, shattered her cheekbone, ricocheted off, and exited through her left nostril. The blood on the gurney in the emergency room had made the wound appear much worse than it was. Only a tiny flap of skin on the side of her nostril was removed by the bullet, and it came out clean, with no bullet bits within. She did not even require surgery. They stopped the bleeding, stitched her up in the rear and front, and left her to heal.

"There was nothing we could do because there was nothing we needed to do," remarked the doctor.

My mum was released from the hospital after only four days. She was back at work in seven minutes.

The physicians kept her sedated for the rest of the day and night so she could rest. They told us everyone to go home. "She's stable," they declared. "You can't do anything here. "Go home and rest." So that's what we did.

I returned to my mother's room first thing the next morning to wait for her to wake up. She was still sleeping when I walked in. Her head was bandaged in the back. She had sutures on her face as well as gauze over her nose and left eye. She appeared thin and weak, exhausted, one of the few times I'd ever seen her look that way in my life.

I sat close to her bed, holding her hand, waiting and watching her breathe, my mind racing with ideas. I was still worried about losing her. I was angry with myself for not being there, and I was angry at the cops for not arresting Abel every time. I told myself years ago that I should have murdered him, which was stupid because I'm not capable of killing someone, but I thought it nonetheless. I was angry at the world, and I was angry with God. Because my mother only prays. If Jesus has a fan club, my mother is unquestionably in the top 100, and this is what she gets?

She finally opened her unbandaged eye after about an hour of waiting. I lost it the moment she did. I burst into tears. She asked for water, so I offered her a cup, and she leaned forward to drink through the straw. I kept weeping, bawling, bawling. I couldn't keep myself in check.

"Shh," she replied quietly. "Baby, don't cry. Shhhhh. "Do not cry."

"How am I not crying, Mom?" "You were on the verge of dying."

"No way was I going to die." I wasn't going to pass away. It's fine. "I wasn't going to perish."

"But I thought you were dead." I couldn't stop crying. "I had thought I'd lost you."

"No way, baby. Don't cry, baby. Trevor. Trevor, pay attention. Take my advice. Listen."

"What?" With tears flowing down my cheeks, I said.

"My child, you must always look on the bright side."

"What? What exactly do you mean, 'the bright side'? You were shot in the face, Mom. There is no silver lining."

"There is, of course. You are now officially the most attractive member of the family."

She burst out laughing with a wide smile. Through my tears, I began to chuckle as well. I was crying and laughing hysterically at the same time. We sat there, she gripped my hand, and we laughed like we usually did, mother and son, through the pain in an intensive-care recovery room on a bright, sunny, and wonderful day.

ENDING

So much happened so soon after my mother was shot. We were only able to piece together the entire event after the fact, after collecting all of the varied accounts from everyone who was present. We had so many unanswered questions while waiting at the hospital that day, such as, "What happened to Isaac?" Where had Isaac gone? We didn't find out till we found him and he told us.

When Andrew drove away with my mother, leaving the four-year-old alone in the front yard, Abel strolled over to his youngest, grabbed him up, and drove away. Isaac looked at his father as they drove.

"Dad, why did you kill Mom?" he said, thinking, as we all did, that my mother was no longer alive.

"Because I'm very unhappy," Abel said. "Because I'm feeling very sad."

"Yes, but you shouldn't murder Mom." "What are we doing now?"

"I'm going to drop you off at your uncle's house."

"And where exactly are you going?"

"I'm going to kill myself."

"But please don't kill yourself, Dad."

"No, I'm not going to kill myself."

The uncle Abel was referring to was a friend, not an actual uncle. He drove away after dropping Isaac off with this friend. He spent the day saying his goodbyes to everyone, family and friends alike. He even told others about what he had done. "This is what I did. I murdered her and am now on my way to murder myself. Goodbye." He spent the entire day on this odd goodbye tour, until one of his cousins finally called him out.

"You need to man up," remarked the cousin. "This is the way of the coward. You must turn yourself in. You had to be a man to accomplish this, and you had to be a man to face the consequences."

Abel broke down and handed over his gun to his cousin, who drove him to the police station where he turned himself in.

He was held in jail for a few weeks while awaiting a bail hearing. We filed a motion to deny bail because he had demonstrated that he was a threat. Because Andrew and Isaac were still juveniles, social services became involved. We thought the case was closed, but then, after about a month, we got a call saying he'd made bail. The big irony was that he was granted bail because he told the judge that if he was imprisoned, he would be unable to support his children. But he wasn't supporting his children; my mother was.

So Abel was no longer present. Everything went against us as the matter moved slowly through the court system. Due to my mother's remarkable recovery, the accusation was reduced to attempted murder. Abel had no criminal record because no domestic violence charges had ever been filed in all of the times my mother had contacted the police to report him. He acquired good counsel, who kept reminding the court that he had children at home who needed him. The matter was never tried in court. Abel entered a guilty plea to attempted murder. He was sentenced to three years probation. He never served a day in prison. He maintained joint custody of his sons. He is free to walk around Johannesburg today. Last I heard, he was still living in Highlands North, not far from my mother.

The final piece of the story came from my mom, who could only tell us her side after she woke up. She remembered Abel pulling up and pointing the gun at Andrew. She remembered falling to the ground after getting shot in the ass. Then Abel came and stood over her and pointed his gun at her head. She looked up and looked at him straight down the barrel of the gun. Then she started to pray, and that's when the gun misfired. Then it misfired again. Then it misfired again, and again. She jumped up, shoved him away, and ran for the car. Andrew leapt in beside her and she turned the ignition and then her memory went blank.

To this day, nobody can explain what happened. Even the police didn't understand. Because it wasn't like the gun didn't work. It fired, and then it didn't fire, and then it fired again for the final shot. Anyone who knows anything about firearms will tell you that a 9mm handgun cannot misfire in the way that gun did. But at the crime scene the police had drawn little chalk circles all over the driveway, all with spent shell casings from the shots Abel fired, and then these four bullets, intact, from when he was standing over my mom—nobody knows why.

My mom's total hospital bill came to 50,000 rand. I paid it the day we left. For four days we'd been in the hospital, family members visiting, talking and hanging out, laughing and crying. As we packed up her things to leave, I was going on about how insane the whole week had been.

"You're lucky to be alive," I told her. "I still can't believe you didn't have any health insurance."

"Oh but I do have insurance," she said.

"You do?"

"Yes. Jesus."

"Jesus?"

"Jesus."

"Jesus is your health insurance?"

"If God is with me, who can be against me?"

"Okay, Mom."

"Trevor, I prayed. I told you I prayed. I don't pray for anything."

"You know," I said, "for once I cannot argue with you. The gun, the bullets—I can't explain any of it. So I'll give you that much." Then I couldn't resist teasing her with one last little jab. "But where was Jesus to pay your hospital bill, hmm? I know for a fact that He didn't pay that."

She smiled and said, "You're right. He didn't. But He blessed me with the son who did."

The contents of this book may not be copied, reproduced or transmitted without the express written permission of the author or publisher. Under no circumstances will the publisher or author be responsible or liable for any damages, compensation or monetary loss arising from the information contained in this book, whether directly or indirectly. .

Disclaimer Notice:

Although the author and publisher have made every effort to ensure the accuracy and completeness of the content, they do not, however, make any representations or warranties as to the accuracy, completeness, or reliability of the content. , suitability or availability of the information, products, services or related graphics contained in the book for any purpose. Readers are solely responsible for their use of the information contained in this book

Every effort has been made to make this book possible. If any omission or error has occurred unintentionally, the author and publisher will be happy to acknowledge it in upcoming versions.

Copyright © 2023

All rights reserved.

Made in the USA
Coppell, TX
11 October 2024

38504886R00075